A Varied Childhood

and

Fifty Years at Sea

by

Captain J. Delaney-Nash F.N.I.

A Varied Childhood and Fifty Years at Sea

copyright © Captain J. Delaney-Nash 2000
revised edition
ISBN 0 907616 43 7

Published in Great Britain by:

Able Publishing
13 Station Road
Knebworth
Hertfordshire SG3 6AP

Tel: (01438) 814316 / 812320
Fax: (01438) 815232

Email: fp@ablepublishing.co.uk
Website: http://www.ablepublishing.co.uk

This autobiography is dedicated to my wife Edith Annie Nash née Garland and Cynthia Gladys Monica Gaydon, my niece, without whose constant encouragement over the years, this book would not have been written. So if anyone does not like the book's contents then please blame them and not me.

I also dedicate this book to the memory of all my Officers and Crew friends of The Eagle Oil Shipping Company Limited, who lost their lives during the Second World War of 1939-1945 pursuing their non-belligerent shipping duties. They were valiant to a man. We shall never forget them.

John Delaney-Nash

The author, Captain John Delaney-Nash FNI,
aged 76 years

A Varied Childhood
and Fifty Years at Sea

This is the Autobiography of Captain John Delaney-Nash FNI. Should you find yourself reading this short story, you may be sure of one thing, everything you read is true and not elaborated upon.

After 50 years in the Merchant Navy I have experienced life in all its many colours, and am thankful for the way fate has treated me, and kept me safe throughout many storms and dangerous tanker operations in peace time and last but not least, six years continuous service in tankers of the "Eagle Oil Shipping Co. Ltd." one of the Shell Mex Group of Companies during World War Two.

I was born in Dublin, Ireland on the 14th June 1910 at 1545 hrs in a small house No. 14 Ruben Street.

My Father was from farming stock, but spent many years in the Army having entered at the age of 16 years. By the time I was born, Dad had completed 22 years service having joined in the year 1888. He joined the Second Battalion of the Essex Regiment known as the "Pompadours", and he was demobbed the year I was born.

My Mother was a young nurse who had trained at the Coombe Hospital in Dublin, which was known as a very fine training centre. She was a dear kind lady who worked at her nursing and spent many hours each day tending her patients. She was well liked by all who knew her. During her long life as a midwife, my Mother had many experiences of unusual and complicated births. She acquired an extensive knowledge of her work and was well liked for her skill by all the various doctors with whom she had worked. During her 50 years as a midwife, my Mother only lost 3 babies and no mothers at all.

In her early years of nursing she often worked long hours day and night, with weekends thrown in for good measure, but when it became time to be paid the patients were so poor that often Mother came home with a pot of jam or pickles or maybe even a chicken, in lieu, if she was lucky. This was in Dublin from 1912 to 1917. Later when the family left Ireland and moved to England in 1917, the same situation often applied in the case of poor patients.

My very first memory as a small child was on the 15th April 1912, when my Mother and I were sitting in St. Stephen's Park in Dublin and heard all the newspaper boys running through the park shouting. My Mother explained to me that a great ocean liner the "Titanic" with hundreds of passengers had sunk to the bottom of the Atlantic Ocean and many people had been drowned. I have a very clear memory of this great disaster, although I don't think I understood the full meaning at the time, but the memory has stayed with me all these years. I am sure there must be some sort of record here as I was only one year and ten months old at the time. I have never forgotten that scene in St. Stephen's Green Park, and my Mother telling me what had happened.

When I was six years old the Irish rebellion was in full swing, that was in 1916. There was fighting in the area and we children had to be kept away from school, to be kept out of danger. My school was badly damaged in the fighting so we had to have our lessons at home with temporary teachers.

We had British soldiers actually firing machine guns in our front garden, where there was a low wall behind which they could take cover from the enemy, i.e. IRA. I can remember my Mother who was a true loyalist, crawling along the front room floor and pushing the window up with a broom handle and handing out mugs of tea and sandwiches to the soldiers in the garden. Many people were killed during the 1916 rebellion, and it was very

6

dangerous to go anywhere near the windows at that time because anything seen moving was immediately shot at. My friend, a little lad of seven years of age, had a little bird which he kept in a small cage on a hook just outside his bedroom window, and at the height of one of these battles he thought his bird might be hurt so he went to the window, opened it and leaned out a little way to reach the cage, and was shot dead. No one ever knew who fired the fatal shot. Anything that moved in the buildings was a fair target.

We lived in a house No. 3 Church Avenue just off the South Circular Road near Dolphins Barn in Dublin. One day a very large detachment of British soldiers were marching towards Rialto and were halted near the end of our road. They were stood at ease and the men just sat down on the pavement to rest and the local people brought them tea and food. My Mother took my sister and I down to the end of the road to see the soldiers. We had only been there a few minutes when shots were fired down the whole length of the road at the soldiers. My Mother hurried off back to our house with me and my sister holding on behind her, to be shielded from the bullets. We got safely back to the house, where we took cover until the fighting stopped. It was quite some time before we children could go back to our schools. The school buildings were damaged and repairs had to be carried out before we were allowed back to our classes. Poor old Dublin was quite badly knocked about during these times and it was dangerous to be out and about in those days. It was a very unsettled period and people of Dublin were relieved when it eased down. There always seems to be trouble in dear old Ireland. One day this wonderful country will settle down and live in peace, and perhaps become rich and prosperous with tourism.

One can dimly remember outings to the seaside at Killiney, Bray, Skerries and Hoath and others which were a bit further inland from the coast. Large parties of us would board big open horse drawn brakes, as they were called, and singing and laughing we would trot along the lanes merrily to our destination, where we would have a grand picnic with plenty to eat and drink. Our destinations were mostly on the coast and our picnics on the sands. At certain times the fish would shoal into the beach driving the whitebait inshore before them, we all ran about in the moonlight and scooped the fish up by the bucketful. I believe the whitebait were being driven inshore by mackerel. Great times were had by all who could join in these parties, and the wonderful sands were ideal for playing games of all kinds, there was no worry of contamination from oil or any other noxious elements. The seas and sands were clean and free from any sort of contamination in those lovely days.

In 1914 the First World War broke out, and life altered for everyone in Great Britain. My Father who had then reached 42 years of age decided to rejoin his old regiment. He was very experienced having fought all through the Boer War in South Africa and on the North West Frontier of India, and had completed 22 years service in 1910.

When the first war broke out, the Commanding Officer of my Father's old regiment wrote to him asking if he would like to come back and rejoin the regiment in his old capacity of Regimental Sergeant Major. The letter from Dad's Colonel reached Dublin two days after my Father had said to my Mother, "I must go back to the Regiment, as they will need all the experienced men they can get, to train all the men that will be required if we are to survive this coming war." My Mother reluctantly agreed, so Dad left for England.

On the day that the letter from the Commanding Officer arrived in Dublin, my Father presented himself before his Colonel and said "I'm back Sir." The Colonel nearly fell off his chair with shock and said "Good God man where have you come from, I only wrote to you a few hours ago!" Of course my Father had never seen the letter having left Ireland before it arrived. As stated my Father rejoined his Regiment in his old rank and went to war.

Dad was wounded twice during the four years of the First World War, the first wound was caused by a bullet which passed clean through his right knee, the second was from a shell explosion and he ended up in Netley Hospital near Southampton. He had shrapnel wounds to his head, face, arms and legs, and the doctors removed 53 pieces from his body. Sometime after he had been released from a Hospital in Glasgow, he was sent to Cambridge to take charge of the training of the Officer Cadet Training Corps and he was still there on the day that the war came to an end on the 11th November 1918 at 1100 hrs.

It was a long time before Dad got over his wounds and really got better, and by that time he was again demobbed and in civvy street.

So many men were now home from the war that work of any kind was hard to find, and my Dad was out of work for over two and a half years before he was given the job as a watchman looking after a hole in the road. Eventually Dad got a job as a Commissionaire - come - porter at the National Physical Laboratory in Teddington, Middlesex, where he stayed until he died in 1945 at the age of 72, near the end of the Second World War. My Father sustained injuries during one of the heavy air raids on Teddington, he was thrown by an exploding bomb head first into an Anderson air raid shelter and suffered a twisted bowel and a severe shaking up. He eventually died of heart valve trouble in January 1945.

During the 1939 - 1945 war my Mother worked through many London air raids in uncomfortable and dangerous conditions. Fate was good to her and she came through without harm. Her patients were her first and last consideration, and she helped many through some rough patches.

9

My Father told us many stories of his life on the North West Frontier of India. The tribesmen were the best fighting men in the world, and my Father respected them as clever and fearless. He told us that when they were on sentry duty at night they stood dead still, and back to back in twos, watching out into the dark black night for the tribesmen who would creep up on them and knife them in the back if they were off their guard. Any movement would disclose their presence to the enemy.

We lived in Ireland, that is Dublin, when the First World War began in 1914, far away from the thought or threat of danger of any sort. It was in Dublin at that time, as a small boy, that I saw for the very first time one of the first great airships. I can't now remember its number but I think it was something like R34 or R101. I am not sure now but it was one of those numbers as far as I can recall.

I first saw Moving Pictures in a cinema called the Camden in about 1915, and they were talking pictures also. They had some kind of speaking tubes around the cinema, and actors or players of some sort spoke and sang and generally accompanied the film and its story.

Sunday was always a great day in Dublin, for our family was a big one and as my Uncle was a butcher we always sat down to a great roast dinner, with all its trimmings. We children sat at a side table and the grown-ups sat together at the main table which was a big one. About 20 people sat down to the meal which always had an air of a special festival about it, and good chatter was enjoyed by all. As children, my sister and I always loved the ride on the tram from Dolphins Barn to Hatesbury Street, the ride was always a great event, and we loved to ride on the top deck which was open, having no roof. One could see the trolley close up and watch the sparks fly off the roller electrode. Sometimes the trolley came off the wire and flew up into the vertical when the power would be lost. The conductor had to get off and pull out from a rack under the tram a long pole with a hook at the end and pull the trolley down and engage it with the power wire once again. With the trolley in place the electric power was restored and the tram was able to proceed on its way.

At one time I remember going into the City of Dublin to Hardcourt Street Station, which was high above the level of the street, to see a railway engine which had failed to stop when entering the station, hanging from its train out of the station having come straight through the wall. It was overhanging the street and resting on a great pile of bricks. I have no idea how they ever got it out of its difficulty. This, as I have mentioned before, was one of the memories I still have of those far off days. I will never forget the great airship gliding silently over the house tops of Dublin, everybody was out in the street looking in wonder at this massive structure. Up until that time no one had ever seen such a large object in the sky. It really looked gigantic because it was flying so low that one could clearly see the people in the gondolas. This period was during the Great War and most of Ireland's young men and a lot of young women too were across the water helping to fight the war. The Irish Regiments gave good account of themselves and were known throughout the world to be brave fighting men. The many Regimental honours of the various Irish regiments are legendary, and their history will live on for ever.

In 1912, to the joy of all, a little sister was born, and they gave her the name of Sheelah, the spelling was taken from one of Moore's poems called "On The Green Banks of Shannon". The poem went something like this:-

On the green banks of Shannon where Sheelah was nigh,
No blithe Irish lad was so happy as I,
No harp like me own could so cheerily play,
And where ever I went was my poor dog Tray.

Poor dog he was faithful and kind to be sure,
And he constantly loved us although we were poor,
When the hard hearted folk, sent us heartless away,
We had always a friend in our poor dog Tray.

At last I was forced from my Sheelah to part,
And she said as the sorrow lay deep in her heart,
Remember me truly when I'm far far away,
And always be kind to our poor dog Tray.

My sister and I had wonderful happy times in Dublin in those days, and we had a dog called Tiny who was a Fox Terrier and loved children. We also had two rabbits who seemed to be part of the family. They were well fed and looked after, and followed us about all over the place. I still have the skin of one of our rabbits, and it is in perfect condition after 72 years.

This song was taught to us at the ripe old age of five years:
The Boer's have got my Daddy
My soldier Dad,
I don't like to hear my Mummy cry
I don't like to hear my Mummy sigh.
So I'm going on a big ship
Across the raging Main,
So I'm going to fight the Boer's I am,
And bring my Daddy home again.

The following song was taught to us at the age of six and a half years of age, in 1916 - 1917:
My Daddy's dressed in Khaki, he's gone away to fight,
For King and Home and Country, for honour and for right.
We do not want the Germans, to come right over here.
So Dad must go and fight them, And he'll beat them never fear.
So we give three cheers for Daddy, we would not keep him back
For we are little Britons, And we love the UNION JACK.

Chapter 2

In 1917 my Dad was working in Cambridge training the Officer Cadet Corps and was based at Trinity College. So now that he was settled into a nine to five job, what could be better than he send for his family to come over to England and leave Ireland for good. This he did and we all came over to Cambridge in late 1917. We crossed from Ireland on a ship called the s.s. "Leinster" which was sunk by German submarines some short time later.

Dad had found us a place to rent on Riverside Drive right on the side of the River Cam. It was a nice house and we could sit in the upstairs window and watch all the river craft moving backwards and forwards, punts, skiffs, canoes and small sailing boats were plentiful and the undergraduates took their lady friends out on the Cam very frequently.

Here now our lives came into order and we were a contented and happy family with a Dad home from the war and a Mum who was once more working as a nurse in the town. My sister Sheelah and I went to Park Street School which was quite near our second home in Cambridge which was situated at No. 12 Portugal Place near the river and also Jesus Green. Later on I went to Milton Road School and my only method of getting there was on roller skates. Most of my friends used roller skates to go to school. There was a nice concrete pathway right across Jesus Green which led to Victoria Bridge, then we had good pathways the rest of the way to school. I was only off my skates when I went to bed and in the house, my Mother insisted I take the skates off in the house but sometimes I forgot and even went up and down stairs on them.

I enjoyed my time in Cambridge very much and we stayed

there for six and a half years, and made a lot of friends. When we finally left Cambridge for Teddington in Middlesex, I thought the end of the world had come, for to leave one's familiar haunts, and one's close friends, never to return was more than a thirteen year old boy and an eleven year old girl could stand. By now we had a young sister, five years old, called Norah Patricia Eveline who was the pride of the family. I also had to give up my scouting, for I was then a member of the 1st Cambridge Sea Scouts, and I was very distressed to leave them.

Going back in time to 1918, when the end of the war arrived, all colleges put on a great Armistice Day Show. There were thousands of undergraduates out in the streets in force and festive mood. Effigies of the Kaiser were burned on great bonfires in the main Market Square and a very hectic time was had by all. The townsfolk joined in the fun and all we kids had an especially good time.

In one case the undergraduates paid a cabby for his cab, they gave him back his horse and tackle, then they filled the cab with anything that would burn. There were firelighters, wood, old boxes, cardboard, broken furniture, and anything that the people had to give that would burn and set fire to the whole lot. They then got between the shafts and pulled the flaming cab, which was an open one and had its top down, throughout the length and breadth of Cambridge and finally back into Market Square where it was added to the great bonfire for a Grand Spectacular. The bonfire was kept going all day by many willing hands.

As I have mentioned before I joined the 1st Cambridge Sea Scouts when I was about nine years old, and also became a member of the choir of All Saints Church in the town. I enjoyed singing and only one thing bothered me. It was one of the rules that each choir boy took it in turn to pump the organ. For a small undeveloped lad this was a mammoth sized job, and one needed plenty of strength to keep the air full up in the bellows. If the music was loud and complicated one could run out of air before the piece of music was finished, with much embarrassment to the organist, so one had to pump like mad to keep the pressure up for the organist to keep going. Many times I thought I would pass out from the strain or that my arms would fall off or both, the fatigue was excessive. However, this must be what is known as growing up, and one somehow managed to fulfil the challenge.

My time in the scouts I enjoyed very much. Our scout hut was on the banks of the Cam, and we learned boating, sculling, canoe work, knots and splicing, camp work and general knowledge about the open countryside, and of course being sea scouts we had to learn to swim and dive and to swim under water. We were also instructed in the art of life saving and first aid and revival of the apparently dead. Camp cooking was also one of our courses and we had to become proficient at cooking a reasonable meal over an open camp fire. Rowing, canoeing and sailing were well practised also. Indoor training consisted of wrestling, boxing, fencing, quarter staff fighting and drills of various kinds. The Kims Game was played very often. It was played as follows: about twenty items were placed on a table, you were allowed 30 seconds to look at them, then they were covered up and each scout had to write down the name of as many articles as they could remember.

We also drilled to the command of "O'Grady Says". If the command was not preceded with the words "O'Grady Says", then one did not obey and stood still without any movement or you were ruled out. If O'Grady said Right Turn, then you obeyed smartly. The last scout to be left on the floor was the winner. This was a very good game, and trained one to keep one's wits alert, and co-ordinate one's senses.

I enjoyed my time in the Sea Scouts in Cambridge and made many friends. Cambridge was a really lovely place to live, and we lived in a house in a paved way called Portugal Place. My youngest sister Norah was born there on the 28th January 1919 and we enjoyed a very happy life there as youngsters in that wonderful old city. In those far off days, it was really a very lovely sight to see the many undergraduates and their lady friends, all beautifully dressed, walking in the town or on the commons or even in their punts, canoes, skiffs, dinghies etc. gliding along the Cam or Backs as that part of the Cam which ran past the rear of the colleges was known. A more tranquil scene one could not imagine, on the warm summer afternoons and evenings.

The chaps wore white open necked shirts, and grey trousers with college blazers and boaters. The young ladies wore lovely flowered and lace hats, almost like sun shades and cool voluminous taffeta and voile dresses. There was a sense of order and gentleness all around, and one felt good and glad to belong. Most people spoke well and tried to pronounce words correctly. The old country accents were there to be heard and one could tell where people came from. Today English is spoken very badly by many people and the pride of tongue has gone by the wayside I'm afraid.

During our six years in Cambridge we enjoyed some very fine summers, and had a very unusual experience of seeing the river Cam run almost dry during a hot summer drought, and at another time we saw the river in full flood, so bad in fact that we had to have all our groceries and milk etc. brought to us by boat. We lowered a cord with a small hook attached from the upstairs window and pulled everything up to the first floor. The ground floors of the house were under about two feet of water. Mud was everywhere and carpets etc. were ruined. How long this state of affairs lasted I can't now remember, but it was a few days. We were all forbidden to go near the river when it was in flood.

We had a sailing dinghy, but I was too young to be allowed out in a sailing craft, that was for the older scouts. Swimming was one thing that was given a great deal of attention, and we were taught to swim properly and learn life saving.

We moved from Riverside Drive to No. 12 Portugal Place close to the town centre, and enjoyed this new accommodation. My sister and I were told never to go near the river, but one day we joined some friends who were going swimming in the river Cam. We had no swimming togs so I remember tying two handkerchiefs together and making myself some swimming shorts. We made something to cover my sister and joined the other kids in the river. We had been in the water for a few minutes when one of the children said "Here comes nurse Nash." Mother wore a long black nurse's cloak and could be recognised a long way away. I swam down the river and hid behind some bushes, but my sister was caught by Mother. She was taken home and given a good thrashing for disobeying orders.

I was so afraid to go home that I hid up in the girders of the Victoria Bridge. I was still all wet and afraid to go home. I saw my father and my Uncle coming across the common towards the bridge, someone must have told my Father where I was, because he called my name and told me to come down at once. Of course I did what I was told and climbed down out of the bridge structure, needless to say my Father just told me how naughty I was and how Mother and friends were very worried about me and my safety, and how much trouble I had caused. Dad never hit me but sent me to bed. He could see how cold I was and both he and my Mother were worried about my health, I had been up in the bridge structure for a couple of hours or more. To cut a long story short, a few days later I developed pneumonia and became dangerously ill. Needless to say like most kids I got better with careful nursing, and was up and about once more in about three weeks. My Mother was not so lucky, she caught the dreaded Spanish Flu and for many days was close to death. After what seemed to be an age, she started to show signs of recovery, and with love and care she slowly regained her health. In those days they didn't have the drugs that we are able to obtain today, and most patients had to fight their own way back to good health, if they were lucky. Pneumonia, Diptheria, Consumption and Scarlet Fever were all known killers in those days. Mother I'm pleased to be able to say fought her way back, right through her serious illness and after some weeks, returned to her buoyant good health once again, much to the relief and joy of all the family.

We had a lovely life in Cambridge and enjoyed the town and surrounding countryside, and to top it all, the people, they were kind and very friendly to us always.

In 1923 the family decided to leave Cambridge because my Dad who had been demobbed twice from the Army after 22 years and another five years in the 1914-1918 war was finally signed off in 1919 from his regiment. Dad found work very difficult to find, men were returning from the war and being demobbed at such a rate that work could not be found for them all.

Chapter 3

My Dad had several jobs but all were of a temporary nature and things were generally very bad in the country. Pay was usually very poor and jobs were few and far between. Dad felt that if he was nearer to London he would have a better chance of getting a position. He was an Essex man born in Onger in 1872, and he felt in these uncertain times he would be better off to stay in England and look for work rather than go back to Ireland. Dad found several jobs but all were very poorly paid and no prospects of any kind were offered. He eventually got a position as a commissionaire at the National Physical Laboratory in Teddington, Middlesex and life for us all started to look up. Mother had been doing lots of nursing work throughout all these years and it was her money that kept our heads above water and assisted us to live in some kind of comfort. Mother got a job in Teddington as a midwife and district nurse, and some time later on was engaged by the Middlesex County Council, as a full time midwife.

I left school, which was a small church school called St. Peter and St. Paul's School at the age of sixteen and a half years and tried for many jobs. I used to sit for hours and answer all sorts of advertisements in the daily newspapers, and although my Dad said I would never get anywhere by writing for jobs, I did at last find myself lucky enough to secure a job as Saleroom Assistant, working for McMeeking and Co., of 10/11 Lime Street, London. The job consisted of going down to the dockland warehouses on the banks of the River Thames in Wapping and Limehouse and surrounding districts and sampling the various chests of tea which had been purchased by my company. There were in the firm's saleroom, one Indian tea buyer, named Mr. Mabley, one China tea buyer whose name I cannot now remember, and Mr. Silvestre the Ceylon buyer for whom I worked. I would be given sheets of paper with a number on each, some consecutive and some not. The name of the warehouse was also on the paper and it was my lot to go to the warehouse indicated and find the consignment. When I found the batch I was looking for I would then get hold of the floor Cooper who would come with me and remove the bung in the tea chest I wished to sample. Using a special tubular phial I would remove a sample of about 2ozs., and make a little parcel of it on the correct numbered paper. The sample was then stowed away in a large canvas bag which we carried on our backs. One can easily imagine that when the bag was almost full of 2oz. samples it was quite heavy, for when the bag was full it held nearly 300 samples about 40 lbs. in weight. The more samples we took the heavier the bag became and still we had long distances to carry it, so the end of the day found us very tired. The visits to the warehouses were an education in themselves. Various teas from all over the world had to be what was called "rebulked". This was a process whereby the tea chests were opened up by a cooper and all the tea emptied out onto the warehouse floor, mixed over and over by a man with a very large shovel and repacked back into the same tea chest. They shovelled the tea back into the same chest, but now that the tea was all loosened up, it would not fit back into the chest, so the cooper had to get into the tea chest and stamp down the tea with his big heavy working boots. He kept adding a little more tea until the original tea all fitted back into the chest. If anyone can imagine 40 or so men all standing in tea chests at one time, and stamping up and down on loose tea, you can see how funny it looked to an observer.

Cutler Street Wharf Warehouse in the centre of London's East End in the vicinity of the Minories was one of the most wonderful places in London to visit. It was a High Value Bond Warehouse, and contained, besides Tea, Coffee, Rubber, some wonderful things such as Perfumes, Spirits, Liqueurs, Spices, Silks, Chinese carpets, Persian carpets and rugs, exotic fruits dried and many other priceless items which came into the country by ships from the Orient. All these items were placed under seal by the Port of London Customs Officers, under whose care they remained, until the merchants who purchased them wished to have them removed to their own warehouses or shops. I was only privileged twice to see the inside of Cutler Street Warehouse but I shall never forget the wonderful smell and appearance of what one can only describe as an Aladdin's Cave.

The samples I was instructed to collect were taken back to our company saleroom and each sample was tested by the buyer, which, as I said, was my direct boss the Ceylon buyer, Mr. Silvestre. Each sample was tested, a kettle of water was boiled and as soon as it boiled the sample of tea was made, if the kettle of water went off the boil it was emptied out and refilled with fresh water, and again brought to the boil, to continue wetting the samples. Several samples of tea were made at one time from each kettle.

The tea was left to infuse for a few minutes by an alarm timer when it was emptied out into special cups, all were arranged in the following manner on the saleroom table:-

1. Box with dry tea leaves.
2. Wet tea leaves on the pot lid.
3. Made tea in the cup-like pot.

The buyer sampled each tea by tasting and spitting out into a spitoon which he pushed along the table from one sample to the next with his foot, examining the dry tea leaf, the wet tea left, and tasting the made sample, there was no milk or sugar used in this operation. This was purely commercial tea tasting in normal practice.

I worked in this tea merchants business for just over one year at a wage of 17/6 per week, eighty five pence new money, and it seemed a bit of a dead end job unless one had a good push from some influential source. Most of the saleroom assistants were public school boys from rich families, so we young chaps had little or no hope of promotion.

My Mother and Father were friendly with a gentleman who worked as an insurance Manager for a shipping firm, and he told them that he could get me away to sea as an apprentice to become a ship's officer. I was asked if I would like to go away to sea, but as I had no knowledge of the sea or anything to do with it I said "No". I'm not really sure now, what happened, but somehow I found myself signing Indentures to serve for four years in the Eagle Oil Shipping Co. Ltd. of 16 Finsbury Circus, London EC3 and on the 21st May 1927, I left my home in Teddington Middlesex for the West India Docks in London, and joined my first ship the 10,000 tonne tanker s.s. "San Silvestre". Strange, wasn't it the name of my first ship being the same name as my old boss Mr. Silvestre.

All during my youth in Teddington I had been a member of the choir of St. Albans Church in Teddington. I had been interviewed by the choirmaster Mr. Alec Rowley, and as I had been in the choir of All Saints Church in Cambridge for some

1913 - 1963

Author's first ship, s.s. "San Silvestre", joined May 1927

three years, I passed the singing test that Mr. Rowley gave me and became a member of the choir of St. Albans Church, Teddington, Middlesex. Choir boys are no different from other boys and any pretty girls in the congregation on Sunday came in for special attention. There was one young and beautiful girl who wore her hair in two long black plaits down her back and who was the centre of attention to several members of the choir. Needless to say I was one of those being most interested in this lovely young girl.

On the Friday morning of the 18th May 1927 I met this lovely lady selling Alexandra flowers outside Teddington Station, and plucking up enough courage I spoke to her. During our conversation I told her that I was joining my first ship on the following Monday morning, and would be away for several months. The name of this very lovely young lady was Miss Edith Annie Garland and I asked her if I wrote to her would she answer my letters. She said she would and this was the beginning of one of the most wonderful courtships one could ever wish to experience. Today, 66 years later, we are still together and love and respect one another in a friendship of close understanding and trust. Except for one occasion when her Mother died, my wonderful companion and sweetheart never missed meeting my ship when we berthed in an English port or a Continental port, which happened on some occasions. I have completed fifty years at sea so there must be a record there somewhere.

Chapter 4

I was an Apprentice in the Eagle Oil Shipping Co. Ltd., one of the Shell Mex Group of companies. I had signed on to do as instructed by my superiors for a period of four years. My pay would be two shillings and sixpence a week for the first two years and five shillings a week for the remaining two years. We also received sixpence an hour for any overtime we had to do.

Life at sea was good but one had a lot of work to do and as a growing boy I found it hard going. The ship's officers were all very good chaps, but one had to obey their every command to the letter, smartly and efficiently, or suffer some kind of punishment which was always a trial or uncomfortable. The hours were long on watch and one did two hours at the wheel, one hour standby and one hour on the lookout. Then we were off watch for four hours and on again for another four hours. This mode of watch keeping was maintained for the duration of the voyage, no matter how long. During the four hours off watch one had to get one's meals, bath and wash oneself, also one's clothing, make and mend and clean the accommodation thoroughly. Sleep had to be worked in where possible. Saturdays were usually used for making and mending and cleaning the half deck which was the name given to the apprentices' accommodation. If we were very lucky and had a really good Chief Officer, we were put on day work. This consisted of being called at six in the morning, turning to at seven and working until eight o'clock, when we had breakfast then turned to again at nine until ten thirty when we had a ten minute break called "Smoke Oh". We resumed work until noon, this was the lunch hour. We resumed work at one o'clock until three, when we had a break for "Smoke Oh", we usually had a mug of tea and a slice of toast which we made ourselves in the galley. The day's work finished at five o'clock, when we washed and bathed ourselves and got into clean clothes. After tea at five thirty we mostly spent the evenings studying, also listening to the radio, and playing darts or deck games, such as deck golf, deck tennis and quoits. During this time we had to keep an ear open for the sound of the Officer of the Watch blowing two blasts on his pocket whistle. This meant that one of the apprentices was wanted on the bridge at once. God help you if you had fallen asleep, for that meant extra work or watch keeping time, which had to be done in one's time off duty. This of course was during one's sleeping time, so one could lose a lot of sleep by not keeping on one's toes all the time. One put in many hours of work during the 24 hours of the full day and sleep was always short and to a young man growing up this was a great physical trial. I have sailed with some Chief Officers or Mates as they are known, who put us on day work from 0700 hrs to 1700 hrs i.e. five o'clock in the evening, then made us split the night between us, on watch on the bridge. That made a 14 hour day for we lads and it was hard going but one had to do it, there was no one to complain to. However, although it seemed very hard treatment and very unjust at the time, it never did any of us a scrap of harm. Here I am today sitting typing this story, I am 84 years of age and can do anything, stay awake for hours if necessary, run, walk, or swim. I bake the bread every fortnight, make chutney, pickles, jam and often cook the meals for my wife and myself, all because of hard upbringing.

Often when the rest of the crew were sitting back enjoying themselves listening to radio, playing musical instruments, playing cards, dominoes or darts and generally having a good time, the Mate often had us boys down the huge Cargo Tanks, cleaning them out with caustic soda, which burned our eyes and skin. The seamen always complained about having to do this rotten job, so to keep everybody happy and complaints to a minimum, we boys always got the job no one else liked.

Most of the Chief Officers were grand chaps, and although they were strict, they were very fair and treated us as human beings, and not just cheap labour as some did. With a good Chief Officer we worked either day work or watch and watch, but never the two together.

The feeding in the Eagle Oil Company was always good, and was known throughout the men of the High Seas, to be the best there was in Merchant Ships. I'm sure they were quite right.

Our menus read something like this:-

Breakfast:-   Porridge
Salt fish
Scrambled eggs
Fruit juice
Bacon and eggs
Bacon and kidneys
Bacon and mushrooms
Fried bread
Flapjacks
Toast and marmalade
Tea or coffee

Lunch:- Joint - Beef, Lamb or Pork
Roast and boiled potatoes
Peas and carrots
Fresh fruit and veg (for a few
    days after sailing)
Various sweets and custard
Plum pudding
Biscuits
Cheese
Coffee

Evening Dinner:- Soup
Roast joint or fish
Roast or chipped potatoes
Various vegetables, mostly tinned
Fruit pies
Fruit tinned
Ice cream
Cheese
Biscuits
Coffee

Supper at 2200 hrs (or 10 pm) when on watch keeping duty:-
Pint mug of tea, coffee or cocoa
Meat, cheese or paste sandwiches. Toast.

On my first trip to sea the Captain was a man of about 54
years of age and named Captain R.Y. Jonnes.

During the voyage out to Tampico in Mexico we saw very
little of the Captain. He never came to meals and never carried
out the usual routine inspections of the ship's quarters and crew
accommodation.

About 19 days out from England, the vessel was about 2 days from Tampico in the Gulf of Mexico, when the Captain came out on deck about 3pm reading the Bible. He was dressed in full black uniform, instead of tropical uniform, as he should have been. He stepped up onto the port railing of the lower bridge and stepped off into the sea. There was a shout of "Man overboard" almost at once from the 2nd Mate who was on watch on the bridge and had heard and seen the man go over the side.

The vessel was turned around and a boat cleared for launching, we steamed back for a period of time and located the lifebuoy that the 2nd Mate had released from the bridge and started a search of the area. We searched around for some considerable time, the sea was unduly calm and oily smooth and there was no wind. After a good length of time spent looking down into the water, the Bosun who was in the bows, shouted out "There he is away down there!" We could all see the Captain deep down in the waters of the Gulf of Mexico. He appeared to be standing straight up in the water. As we watched we realised that the body was coming slowly to the surface. After some considerable time the Bosun using a boat hook caught the Captain by the collar of his jacket and slowly pulled him to the surface.

We got the Captain out of the water and laid him in the bottom of the boat. It is strange to say, but the Captain and his body were as black as a Negro's. We found later that he had a large protrusion over the area of his heart, as if he had had a spear pushed through his body from the back. The skin wasn't broken but the protrusion on his chest looked like a huge boil, we never discovered what it was, some said his heart had burst, but I never found out.

We landed the Captain in Tampico where he was buried,

some members of the crew attended the ceremony. It took some little time for the Authorities to prepare the necessary paperwork and prepare all the documents that were required by Mexican law, so the ship was delayed about 48 hours or so. The Chief Officer took command and we completed the voyage under his authority. We found out after checking the ship's bond that 40 bottles of whisky had been consumed by the Master in 19 days.

On the day he committed suicide myself and my chum the senior apprentice had spent the afternoon doing our washing. We had just finished hanging the things on the line out on the Main Deck when the Captain came on deck and without any warning, started shooting at us with a Webley 45mm hand gun. My pal and I both ducked behind the Summer Tank Hatches and hid out of sight, my pal said "He has only two bullets left, as soon as he has fired off the other two, run aft as fast as you can and get under cover before he can reload." This we did and we found out later that the Captain was not shooting at us, but at all our clothes on the clothes line, which he seemed to think were people. Later when we took our washing in from the clothes line, we found 5 bullet holes in our clothes. He was obviously quite able to shoot straight.

On one occasion I was appointed to the job of overseeing the building of a new ship in Haverton Hill on Tees. The ship was called the s.s. "Empire Grenadier" an 18,000 ton tanker belonging to the Eagle Oil Shipping Co. Ltd. As it was wartime we had to do our speed trials alongside the quay in the fitting out basin. Huge spring-type meters were placed between the ends of our mooring ropes and the mooring bollards on the quayside. Our engines were worked at Slow, Half and Full Speeds both ahead and astern. The readings were taken by the Naval Architects and our speeds calculated accordingly. All the superstructure was being welded by young men and women of about 18 years of age.

I'm afraid they didn't know very much about welding, and after we got to sea we found out how much they really didn't know. The first really heavy sea we shipped struck the fore and aft bridge and about 100 feet of the safety railing came right away and landed on the main deck below.

Halfway across the Atlantic on our way to New York the spare propeller broke adrift. This was a very serious matter, because the propeller weighed about 25 tons. We used heavy blocks and tackles and big wooden wedges to make the propeller fast once more, but I had to have men watching the whole time, and the ship's carpenter spent his time hardening up the wooden wedges as they worked loose as the vessel rolled in the rough seas. When we got to New York the welders from the Dry Dock in Brooklyn had a really good laugh at what we called "welding". They said "No way was that welding!" They said it was what they called "spot" welding.

Real welding is building up the original metal to its previous size and making it stronger than it was before. After they had re-welded all the necessary work, it never came apart again. As it was wartime, ships were being repaired and built as fast as the work could be done, and of course many unskilled people were being used to help speed up the job. The Germans were sinking many ships and building was at full pressure in all the world's ship yards.

Work was going on apace in all the ship yards of the world and any labour they could get was used to help in the construction of ships of all kinds, to assist in the war effort. Hundreds of tons of shipping was sent to the bottom of the world's oceans by the Germans. Their "U" boats were everywhere. Many seamen were drowned between 1939 and the end of the war in 1945. It was a long war and everyone was tired and looked forward to its end.

The Americans were building ships at a most impressive rate, and replacing the ships that were being sunk by new tonnage, this went on all through the war. The ships were basic but nevertheless they filled the gap and helped the allies to win the war in the end.

I, personally, lost many good friends in the war, and could never understand how I was able to go through it without any harm to myself. I spent four and a quarter years carrying Aviation Spirit and Motor Gasoline across the Atlantic and saw many ships sunk in my convoys, but I came through without hurt. In one convoy a ship close ahead of us was torpedoed and as she was loaded with a full cargo of some sort of petroleum spirit, swung across our course, exploded in the centre and the two halves parted company and went off in opposite directions. My ship, which had no time to avoid the two halves as they blew apart from each other, went straight through the gap and came out on the other side unscathed, even though we also were also loaded with Aviation Spirit. The heat from the burning ship was so hot that it scorched our eye lashes and brows and all the hair below our hat bands.

We saw members of the crew running around the decks all on fire, some of the jumping into the sea where they perished in the flaming water. Very few of the crew were saved, I believe now that the ship in question was Norwegian registered.

On one voyage when we were returning home from Mexico, we encountered very heavy weather in the North Atlantic Ocean. A very high sea was running from the north west and the ship was labouring somewhat.

s.s. "SAN FABIAN" - Tranquil days in the South Atlantic, 1938

Our 3rd Steward was taking some vegetables along the fore and aft bridge from amidships to the ship's galley which was situated aft on the starboard side. He was halfway along the bridge when he saw out of the corner of his eye, a mighty wave breaking over the port quarter, he turned away from the great wave and hung onto the railing as tight as he could. The sea crossed over the vessel and after what seemed to be an age, a shout from the bridge "There's a man down in the water at the forward end of the Main Deck." Yes, it was the 3rd Steward.

Several men got the steward up to the hospital on the starboard side of the accommodation, where he was examined for injuries. He was quite unconscious, very cold and bleeding from various places here and there, large bruises were coming up on his body as he was being examined.

We had to land the steward in Fayal in the Azores, and I, the 3rd Officer, had to go ashore with him to hand him over to the Hospital Authorities, where he remained for six to eight months.

We found out later that the young steward's jaw was broken in five places and he had nearly been cut in half by the weight of the wave forcing him down across the one and a quarter diameter iron railing which we found later was bent to the shape of his body. He was vomiting up bucketfuls of jade green bile every few hours, his internal organs must have been in a terrible state.

The 3rd Steward was finally discharged and sent home from hospital D.B.S. "Distressed British Seaman". The poor lad was only home for a few months when he shot himself. He suffered more than anyone realised.

One thing that was always drummed into we boys, by the senior officers, was how to look after ourselves on deck in heavy weather. We were taught to read the sea, its direction and speed of travel, and judge when to dodge from one place of safety to another, always looking for something strong to hang on to. Judgement in timing the seas coming board was a thing to be learned for one's own safety. As much shelter as possible must be sought, it is impossible to hold on to any structure in the full force of a big wave. No matter how strong a man might be he could not overcome the force of water in a big wave coming over the decks. The seamen should be instructed to keep off the decks in heavy weather, their own safety is paramount.

On one of our voyages out to Mexico, we carried six passengers, who were company personnel bound out to work in Curacao and Aruba. The six were one married couple, three men and one woman.

During the trip the officers decided to give a party and put on an evening of dancing and refreshments. The poop deck was suitably decked out in coloured bunting and coloured lights. We, the two apprentices, were not invited to the celebrations probably because we were watch keeping and not getting too much sleep.

The dancing was at its height when the Senior Apprentice said we should go along aft and peep in on the frivolities. This we did, and made our way along aft and climbed up onto the fiddley tops, from where we could look down on the deck below and watch the dancing without being seen.

The 3rd Engineer was dancing with the Chief Engineer's wife and seemed to be having a good time. We lads were always playing tricks on the 3rd Engineer and he was often the butt of our fun. This night was no exception and the Senior Apprentice whom we will call "Tom", took from the nearby potato locker, a nice round potato, about the size of a billiard ball, which he said he was going to throw at the 3rd Engineer.

Because we were in total darkness on the fiddley tops with bright lights all round the poop deck no one could see Tom and I at all. As the 3rd Engineer and the Chief's wife danced into shot distance, Tom threw the potato just at the moment when the 3rd Engineer swung his partner around. Yes, you have it - the potato hit the Chief Engineer's wife in the right temple. She let out a small cry and dropped to her knees half stunned, and we ran.

We knew we were in serious trouble if we were found out and caught. We couldn't take the risk of being seen jumping down from the fiddley tops, so our next best bet was to climb up the Main Funnel Ladder to the Whistle Platform. This we did, and took refuge 54 feet above the Poop Deck, from where we could see all the people running around and flashing torches looking for the villains who had made the attack. We stayed up the funnel for some considerable time, until we saw the people gathering on the after end of the Poop Deck, then we hastened down the funnel and ran along the main deck and ran into the accommodation, or the Half Deck as our quarters were known. We slipped into our pyjama jackets and jumped into bed feigning sleep. A little time later we heard someone say, "Let's look in here." Then the lights came on. My chum and I looked out from under the bed clothes and anxiously asked "What's up?" The Chief Officer, Chief Engineer and 3rd Engineer looked at each other and said "They're not involved." They then put out the lights and went on deck.

I am pleased to say that they never found out who threw the potato, they would have given us a good hiding, if they had only guessed. Needless to say we were very sorry that the so called prank had gone all wrong and we were pleased to know that the Chief Engineer's wife was not really hurt.

It's a strange thing, but as one sits and continues writing, various other stories come into one's mind. Most of them have been long since forgotten and for no real reason pop up in one's memory quite fresh and in great detail.

This story is one such. When our ship left England bound for the West Indies and places afar, it was our custom as soon as we were reaching the lower latitudes and the weather was getting warmer, to rig up the swimming bath. This bath was constructed of 9" x 3" x 7' planks, and when all was put together formed a box 21' 6"x 12' x 7' deep, this box was lined out inside with a canvas lining of the same size, and held when filled about 50 tons of sea water.

One morning we were in the swimming bath having a competition to see how many metal ashtrays we could bring up from the bottom in one go. During this game the 2nd Engineer who was struggling to retrieve the ashtrays, kicked me in the right ear with the ball of his heel with some force. Some time later when I was in front of the mirror in my cabin combing my hair and having a cigarette in my lips I sneezed, and saw to my amazement, smoke puffing straight out of my right ear. I found, by taking a mouthful of smoke and keeping my lips tight closed, and holding my nose, I could force the smoke out of my ear.

I went to the Captain and told him what had happened, and of course he asked for a demonstration there and then, this I duly complied with and it was funny to see the look on the Captain's face when he saw the smoke spurt out of my ear.

The Captain said after he had overcome his astonishment, "You must come ashore with me when we arrive in Santos tomorrow morning and see the Company Doctor. We arrived in Santos at 1000 hrs the next morning, and when the Captain left the ship to visit the Agent I went with him. The Agent took the Captain and I to see the

Doctor, who was Japanese, and once again I gave my demonstration.

The Doctor was not very impressed and gave me some drops to put in my ear. He said it would take about six days to repair. He was quite right and in six days after treatment I could no longer perform my party piece. My hearing became normal and has remained so ever since.

When we were about to leave the surgery the Doctor said to the Captain, "Captain you seem to be very hard of hearing. I would like to examine your ears." The Captain agreed and the Doctor instructed the nurse to put some drops into his ears. About 30 minutes later the Doctor returned to examine the Captain's ears and using a probe and tweezers he removed from each ear a cotton wool plug about one and a quarter inches long that had been put there many years before when the Captain was about 11 or 12 years of age. It was well known to everyone in the Eagle Oil Fleet and in its office that the Captain was very deaf, but nobody ever stumbled upon the real reason.

We, that is the officers and apprentices, who lived on the deck directly below the Captain's accommodation always enjoyed a sing song or the playing of musical instruments generally during the Dog Watches in the evening. This we often did but without disturbing the Captain in any way.

After leaving Santos the story was quite different because the Captain could now hear a pin drop three decks down. His hearing became acute and although we were all very pleased for him, it cut our noise limits well down and we had to exercise more consideration during the evening hours.

During our voyages from the Caribbean to South America and back, we had a period where we took to writing poems. Here are a few of these poems:-

West Indies To The River Plate

Bound North for Curacao me lads, in May of thirty eight,
Bound North for Curacao me lads, in ballast from the Plate.
Four trips South ahead of us, just days of work and toil,
Painting up the ship me lads, and working Shell Mex Oil.

Our days are long and tedious, but still we never grumble,
We say aye aye, and show a leg as out of bed we tumble,
We're called at any time at all, to be ready for the fray,
The tugs are here, the Pilot too, we're making port today.

Our Captain's name is Davis and Hawkins is our Mate,
Years up and down this coast they've been, trading to the Plate.
Buenos Aires, Montevideo, two cities full of fun,
With pretty girls to welcome us when we have made the run.

Aruba Sir; there's nothing there, just miles of waste and sand,
The North East Trades keep blowing Sir; just blow to beat the band,
The sand just cuts your face and legs, and spoils our bit of fun,
Or else we'd get good bathing Sir, beneath the blazing sun.

Now this is all I have to say about this run out here,
We do not mind it very much so long as there is cold beer,
Or half a pint of Vino Red to war our Mary Ann,
Then we will sail the seas for months, in the good San Fabian.

J. Delaney-Nash
s.s. "San Fabian"
1938 - 1939.
South Atlantic.

39

She was homeward bound from Mexico,
Her last trip some did say,
And why not, she is old and worn
And sure has earned her pay.

She steams through Atlantic's wintery seas,
Homeward for her well earned rest,
She's signing off with a good DIS A,
For the company's had of her best.

She's done twenty years of long hard toil
Bringing home the Shell Mex Oil,
And now they know her time is done
And her pension due and her long rest won.

We've been to Valpo alas and alack,
In quarantine with Yellow Jack,
Four men ill and one man dead,
Hell of a trip the Old Man said.

And that's not all the Second laughed,
We've found a crack in the tailend shaft,
The crack was right across the coupling,
So they shrunk on a band to stop it buckling.

She's chugging home at an average nine,
Through moderate seas with the weather fine,
So now's the time to chip and paint,
Make her look real good though she jolly well ain't.

J. Delaney-Nash
3rd Officer
s.s. "San Valerio"
South Atlantic 1934.

Three monkeys sat in a coconut tree.
Discussing things as they're said to be.
Said one to the others, "Now listen you two,
There's a certain rumour that can't be true
That man descended from our noble race,
The very idea is a disgrace.

No monkey ever deserted his wife,
Starved her babies and ruined her life;
And you've never known a mother monk
To leave her babies with others to bunk,
Or pass them on from one to another
Till they scarcely know who is their mother.

And another thing you'll never see,
A monk build a fence round a coconut tree
And let the coconuts go to waste,
Forbidding all other monks to taste,
Why, if I put a fence round a coconut tree
Starvation would force you to steal from me.

Here's another thing a monk won't do;
Go out at night and go on a stew,
Or use a gun or club or knife
To take some other monkey's life.
Yes, man descended, the ornery cuss,
But brother, he never descended from us".

Anon.

THE LITTLE MONARCH

There was a little Monarch who sat upon a throne,
And as he was a bachelor he had to sit alone,
He tried to find a lady to sit along with him,
So one fine day he doffed his hat to a girl called Mrs. Sim.

Said he "I'm very lonely upon my golden throne,
Because I want you only, for my very own.
I know you're over forty, but I am forty three,
Though people say you're naughty you're quite O.K. with me."

Said she "Alas I'm married but my husband is a clown,
Oh, how I wish I'd tarried for I long to wear a crown."
The little Monarch looked annoyed then said "I know a Man,
Who'll make your marriage null and void." And to the court he
ran.

The judge put on his wig and gown and said "the case is clear,
Your husband bars you from the Crown, I'll soon fix that my
dear,"
He straight way granted a divorce, ne'er asking for causation,
Then timed it to come into force before the Coronation.

The lovers were elated to name the happy day,
When they would both be mated with none to tell them nay.
Just then the voice of Stanley B. rang out so stern and clear,
"You may do that in U.S.A., but you can't do that there 'ere."

J. Delaney-Nash
South Atlantic
March 1937

My very first voyage was over four months long and although I came back to Old Kilpatrick on the River Clyde in Scotland, I was unable to get home to Teddington, and was therefore not able to see my new girlfriend, Miss Edith Garland. We sailed outwards from Scotland for Tampico in Mexico where we loaded a full cargo of motor spirit for Shell Haven in the Thames. On our arrival in Shell Haven the Senior Apprentice and myself the Junior Apprentice were put on a very dirty job of coaling the Galley Bunkers. The coal was hauled up the ship's side in wicker baskets, from barges tied up alongside, one can imagine the state we got into, we were black with coal dust from head to toe, and this was the position we were in when one of the stewards came to inform me that my Mother and new girlfriend were coming along the jetty on a visit to the ship. Needless to say I hadn't the time to get properly cleaned up before I met them, and of course I really wanted to impress my new girlfriend. Well Mother and Edith were so pleased to see me, that my by now half washed condition was accepted as part of the scene. From that day onwards with only one exception when her Mother died, my sweetheart was always on the quayside to meet my ship on our arrival. We were always very close and very much in love with each other and on the 8th December 1937 we were married in St. Albans Church, Teddington, Middlesex. A great day still well remembered.

We spent our Honeymoon in Bournemouth, and although it was December and everywhere was covered with snow, we had a wonderful time.

We had made no plans for the Honeymoon, so after the wedding we took the train from Teddington to Waterloo, and on Waterloo Station there was a town plan of Bournemouth in a huge glass case, showing all the streets and town buildings.

We had a good look at it and I asked my new wife if she had ever been to the resort of Bournemouth and she said she had not, so we decided to go there for a week. We stayed the night in an hotel in London and the following day we took off for Bournemouth. The journey down was a picture, the whole countryside was deep in snow, so heavy that the telephone wires were hanging in great bights nearly touching the hedge tops along the way.

We stayed at the Beach Cliffe Hall Hotel, which we found quite by luck. It was a very good hotel, warm, friendly and the food was super.

During the day we went for walks in the town and on the front and spent the evenings cuddling and making love. The days flew by and I was soon back at sea again, many dreadful partings we had to experience during my 24 years away deep sea. After joining British Rail and serving on the cross channel steamers, we never looked back, and were never parted for more than a few days ever again.

Just before our wedding we went to Richmond in Surrey to buy some furniture for our new home, a rented house in Teddington which we shared with my new Mother-in-Law who was a dear kind lady who had our future happiness and prosperity uppermost in her mind. We had very little money at that time, somewhere about £300 but not much more, of course that was a good sum in those days. I well remember spending £148 in the first furniture shop we dealt with, and because we were such good customers and had spent so much money with them, they invited us i.e. my wife and I to a full meal up in their Restaurant all free of charge. Needless to say we spent more money with them later on in our married life.

We bought our home bit by bit and I'm sure we loved it and all its bits and pieces, because each piece of our belongings represented a positive step in our lives which we can both remember in detail. We lived in happiness and harmony with my Mother-in-Law until she died in 1949. I was by now a Captain in the Eagle Oil Shipping Co. Ltd. and earning a good salary. Life was good and we had a nice home and I think the fact that we had no children drew us closer together as the years went by. We have had our Golden Wedding and are now in our eighties and both very fit and enjoying life still.

All the Officer's wives were allowed to stay onboard the ship until we cleared outwards for a foreign port, so very many happy hours were enjoyed by all. No children were born to us so we grew very close together and hated it when we were forced to part.

Even though we were parted from each other for long periods, life at sea was a wonderful experience for anyone. We young men had plenty of work to do in our different capacities according to our ranks, but we were not working all the time. Hours were spent sitting out on deck talking or reading or just watching the sea pass by, and enjoying the lovely warm breeze and sunshine when we were in the tropics. We played many deck games and as soon as we entered the fine weather zones, we rigged up a portable swimming bath and had great fun and exercise in that. The bath was 18' long and 12' wide and 7' deep, so we had plenty of room for diving and swimming. Evenings off duty were given over mostly to studying.

Six to eight in the evenings, was the time for indoor games and at eight o'clock all noise of any sort was frowned upon, because the men who were due to keep the midnight to four a.m. watch went to sleep then. It was looked upon as a serious action to wake the middle watch members from their well needed sleep, this watch was always known as the Grave Yard Watch. Studying was of great importance as one needed to work hard for one's certificates on the way to Command. One could go on for writing for many pages on our days at sea, some good and some very dangerous when the weather was extremely bad, sometimes for days on end. On many occasions the Captain had to nurse the vessel through very rough and heavy seas and he had to remain on the bridge for many hours.

I have crossed the Atlantic well over a hundred times and have been up and down the South Atlantic and the West Coast of South America on many, many occasions. If you take an atlas of the world, then I will have been to some place on every page.

On one occasion when we were bound up in the Mississippi on our way to a place called Norco, some few miles above Baton Rouge. The river was flowing very fast, we were only making about four knots over the ground when at one of the bends in the river we nearly had a collision with a seaplane which was flying down the river just a few feet above the surface. The pilot of the plane saw us just in time and went into a steep climb, just missing our foremast by what looked like a few inches.

The Mississippi is a very fast flowing river, the water would lap the top of the levee. Way back in the 1920s the townspeople of New Orleans used to place guards along the top of the levee, to keep watch for the farmers from the other side of the river, who would come over in the night and blow a hole in the levee, which would make a breach in the bank on the townside rather than have the crops ruined by the flood water on the farmside.

The guards on the levee would shoot anyone they could make out approaching the river levee under cover of darkness. One can understand their concern, but I am afraid not their methods. They had no consideration for the town which might be flooded for days on end.

In dense fog, the Mississippi pilots navigated the river by blowing short blasts on the ship's whistle every few minutes. They could tell by the time taken for the whistle blast to rebound from each of the river banks, whether the ship was in the middle of the river or not. This was long before the advent of radar and electronic sounding machines and instruments. Nevertheless the pilots managed very well and kept their ships afloat even in the most restricted of visibilities. The Americans always seemed very casual in their manner, but I have always found them very fine seamen in all respects and under all conditions. During the last war when I worked very closely with them as members of the American Pacific Fleet off Japan for over two years, I found them calm, efficient and considerate, discipline on their ships was more strict than that to be found on British ships. No intoxicating drink was allowed on American vessels and although their manner seemed to us to be very casual they were "on the ball" at all times, they were great chaps all of them.

I have made many trips to Tampico and Minatitlan in Mexico and I loved the Mexican people. They were kind and helpful to us whenever we needed any advice. The country was pretty wild when I first went there in June 1927. I remember being introduced to a man who had just murdered another man, away up country, because he tried to rape his cousin. He said he had come away until the trouble had blown over. Sanitation and the roads were very primitive and the buildings all seemed to need painting, but in the wonderful weather, no one seemed to worry.

It was during my first two years at sea as an apprentice that we experienced some very heavy weather. It must have been about the years 1928 to 1934. I can't remember the details now but as we were returning to England from Mexico, and about 1200 miles from the Fastnet Lighthouse on the S.W. corner of Ireland, we experienced some very very rough and heavy weather. The Atlantic Ocean was suffering one of its really bad spells. We were having a very difficult time in mountainous seas, and as we were loaded, we were like a half-tied rock and most of the time were buried under gigantic waves. We received several distress messages from nearby ships. During this time the "Saxilby" (15.10.1933), "Millpool" (3.10.1934), "Ainderby" (10.6.1934 - torpedoed) and a German ship called the "Isis" which was on her maiden voyage, were all sunk. The loss of life was very heavy, so I believe. The "Isis" was only a few miles ahead of us when her Radio Officer signalled for help. Her call lasted only a few minutes and was never heard again. Her hatches were stove in and she went straight to the bottom.

The story went that the apprentice was sent to get one of the lifeboats ready for launching and he was in the boat when it was snatched out of the davits as the vessel plunged down into the deep. The apprentice was the only survivor from this unlucky ship, he must have had a charmed life. We heard later on, that a high ranking German Naval Officer, heard of this young lad's ordeal and took him under his wing, and had him educated to be a Naval Officer in the German Navy. As this is only hearsay, I can't be sure, but that was the story that went around at the time.

Some of my facts may not be quite accurate because time dims one's memory. It is now 62 years since these experiences, so I must be excused a few misquoted dates.

I served on several vessels of the Eagle Oil Shipping Co. Ltd. They were all tankers of about 10,000 to 25,000 tons and one day when I was in our London Office at 16 Finsbury Circus, London, I asked our Personnel Clerk Mr. Grabble if he was trying to kill me. In much surprise he asked me what I meant, I told him that I had been carrying clean oil i.e. petrol and aviation spirit across the Atlantic Ocean for four and three quarter years in a dangerous war and had he never heard of the old saying about "going once too often to the well?" He immediately got my meaning, and said he would try and appoint me to a nice Black Oil ship.

Black heavy fuel oil was supposed to be much safer than spirit cargoes. He told me to go home, have a good leave and he would see what he could do. Sure enough he was as good as his word and after about three and a half weeks' leave he appointed me to a ship called the m.v. "San Adolfo" a 12,000 ton black oil tanker, which was fitting out in the Middle Docks in South Shields on the River Tyne.

On joining the ship and seeing all the unusual work being carried out, I asked the Master, one Captain Archer, O.B.E. what it was all about. Captain Archer was an old personal friend of mine and we had sailed together two or three times before. As I was now his First Mate or Chief Officer, I felt a bit out of my depth with all this unfamiliar equipment and fittings. Captain Archer laughed and said "It's easy to see you haven't done any oiling at sea, John, you see we are fitting out to act as a fleet oiler and supply vessel." He also told me that he had no idea where we were due to do the refuelling, or what our future orders were likely to be.

A great deal of work was going on during the day but the evenings were mostly to ourselves. My wife was onboard all the time during our refit and life was made the most of generally.

Chapter 5

In September 1939 the Second World War broke out, and our lives changed to one of worry for our families and each other's safety generally.

In July 1939 I had undergone a course of gunnery on board H.M.S. "President" in the River Thames, and in August I joined the m.v. "San Eliseo" as Second Officer and Gunnery Officer and sailed in one of the first convoys of the war. Seafaring took on a much more sinister look for all sailing at sea. We went out to America and the Gulf of Mexico for our cargo of motor spirit and aviation fighter spirit. Known to all as "clean oil ships". I carried many thousands of tons of this spirit across the Atlantic Ocean for four and three quarter years. Some of the following stories may give you an idea of what the job was like sailing the High Seas in these long gone days.

We left Avonmouth on the night of the 8th April 1943 in the s.s. "Empire Grenadier" a wartime built tanker of some 18,000 tons burden, joining in convoy with vessels of all types and sizes, leaving Barry Roads for the United States of America and orders.

We had been instructed by the Naval Commodore at the Convoy Conference that submarines would be our greatest danger on this coming voyage to the United States of America and that it would be imperative to keep close formation, and well closed up in our respective positions, thereby giving the Naval Escort a better chance to cover the convoy without too large an area to patrol. We formed convoy soon after leaving the Bristol Channel and proceeded south of Ireland out into the Atlantic Ocean. The weather was clear but heavily overcast which was to our advantage, as it was poor flying weather for the Germans and their planes working out of France endeavouring to harass British and Allied shipping where and when possible.

The voyage was fairly uneventful well out into the Atlantic, owing no doubt to the mixed bag of weather we were experiencing. By the time the convoy reached 35 degrees West Longitude the weather had deteriorated to low cloud, heavy rain and wind increasing to about force 9 or 10 with a rough sea and a heavy swell. The "Grenadier" was gradually becoming more lively and less comfortable.

Night was closing in and the ships of the convoy were beginning to fade into the background of darkness. No lights of any sort were being carried, not even the regulation shaded blue stern light was permitted, and only the dark outlines of the convoy ships were visible to those, who after four years of war and convoy work, had the vision of night owls.

All instructions for the night such as zig zag patterns to be carried out during the night, alterations of courses, alterations of clocks and any other required orders, had to be passed by morse or flag signalling during the afternoon watch. Therefore there was no necessity to show lights of any sort during the hours of darkness. Once night had closed in then lights of any type were taboo, the smallest glimmer of light was a menace to any convoy on the high seas, as the officers and ratings in enemy craft and submarines were trained to spot even the dimmed light from a compass shining on the face of the officer of the watch, when he was engaged in taking a compass bearing at night. All ship's side ports, windows and openings were blanked off and all doors which opened out onto decks were fitted with door switches, which cut off the electricity as the door was opened. The heat in the enclosed spaces, such as the engine room and boiler rooms etc. was very uncomfortable, owing to the blackout, skylights and vents were fitted with blanks to eliminate light. Engine room officers and ratings found the night hours on duty long and very tiring, due to the close damp heat. Mornings and the opening up of doors, ports and skylights to the available fresh air were welcomed by all.

The darkness on the bridge was almost total by now, and only the faint outline of the officer on watch, the man at the wheel, and the apprentice on the bridge wing could be seen by those whose eyes were accustomed to the deep darkness. Outside on the bridge wings the lookouts were just visible against the black curtain of the night sky.

At about this time the Engine Room Telegraph rang shattering the stillness in the wheelhouse, and causing the Chief Officer to jump to the telegraph to see it reading "Stop" which he promptly answered, ordering the apprentice to call the Captain to the bridge at once. The apprentice blew down the Captain's speaking tube almost before the Chief Officer had finished speaking, and was heard passing the information to the Captain. Within three minutes of the telegraph ringing "Stop" the Captain arrived on the bridge and told the Chief Officer to enquire from the Chief Engineer what was the reason for the "Stop". By this time the vessel was losing headway and slowly dropping astern of the convoy, and was also beginning to lose steerage way. At about this time the Radio Officer came into the wheelhouse and handed the Chief Officer a radio signal, from the Commodore of the Convoy. The signal read "All ships. Keep well closed up. Wolf Pack of submarines shadowing the convoy. Message ends."

As the Captain read the message in the charthouse the Chief Engineer put his head round the wheelhouse door, and to everyone's amusement said "Is there anyone there?" Coming straight along from the bright lights of the engine room, his eyes were unaccustomed to the dense blackness of the wheelhouse and could see nothing at all, though everyone in the wheelhouse could clearly see him.

The Chief Engineer was taken into the charthouse to the Captain, where he informed the Captain that the main engine had stopped because a small roller which was part of the governor system had split and dropped out of the engine. There was no spare part and before the engine could be restarted it would be necessary to make a new part and how that was to be done, he, the Chief Engineer, did not know, as there was no lathe and only a few tools of any sort on board the vessel.

Within about half an hour of stopping the convoy was about five miles ahead and the "Empire Grenadier" was wallowing like a sitting duck in a heavy sea and increasing swell, with high winds and very heavy rain. We were waiting every moment for the deafening explosion which would tell us one and all, that we had been found and sorted out with much rejoicing among the officers and ratings of an enemy U-boat.

The only sounds that could now be heard on the ship, was the sound of sea water breaking over the decks, striking the ship's side and spilling off back into the sea. During this time the situation was being assessed and attacked by our Second Engineer one Mr. George Gibb, who was engaged in putting on his thinking cap and trying to see what he could do to solve this problem of life and death. With the aid of an industrial Wolf drill, clamped in a vice and using a series of files of different shapes, he was endeavouring to make a new roller.

It is a well known thing, that our Marine Engineers, as nearly all enlightened seafarers know, have a happy knack of coming up with the goods, when all seems to be lost and odds are heavily stacked against one. This I am pleased to say was the case in this very dangerous situation and believe it or not, a new piece was made under the most primitive conditions, fitted into its vital position in the main engine, a Poppet Valve type machine and to everyone's astonishment worked without any further trouble.

At about 0250 hrs the vessel got under full speed and commenced zig zagging her way back to the long gone convoy.

At 1620 hrs the next day of this memorable epic the s.s. "Empire Grenadier" took up her station in the west bound convoy and received a signal from the Commodore of the convoy saying "Well done 43, please resume your station."

Ingenuity and an anxious night slogging against time, by our Second Engineer, saved a great tanker and all her very grateful crew. If we had been unable to get moving before dawn, we would have been torpedoed and sunk with little chance of rescue, of this there is no doubt.

On one occasion during 1944 I took a cargo of aviation spirit to the town of Pozzuoli just north of Naples. We sailed around the south of Sicily and through the Messina Straits on the way to the Port of Naples and strange to say we had the very unusual experience of seeing Mount Etna, Stromboli and Vesuvius all in eruption and pouring out flames, rocks and dust in large quantities. It was a sight to see, how often this sort of display takes place I don't know, but it was well worth seeing - the year was 1944.

During the war we were always being told by the Commodores of the many convoys we sailed in to keep well closed up in our places in the convoys. The reason for this was that the escort vessels could protect us, without having too large an area to cover, so "keep close up" was the order of the day and night.

Our Captain was a Cornishman and built like the trunk of an oak tree, and was very precise in all he did, and the Commodore's word was the law as far as he was concerned. So much so that on one occasion when we were steaming up the North Sea on our way to Newcastle-upon-Tyne, and proceeding along E-boat Alley, as it was called, we were attacked by German aircraft. High velocity bullets were flying all over the place and everyone was busy trying to get a shot at the planes flying through the night sky, when we heard a voice from inside the wheelhouse saying "Never mind the Germans Mister, where's the ship ahead?" It was obvious that station keeping was the uppermost thing in the Captain's mind. I have always thought that this sort of thinking is very British and what makes the Britisher so strong in adversity.

The following accounts may be of some interest to the reader, so I just intend to enter these thoughts as they come into mind.

Many years ago when we were homeward bound from Mexico, and steaming home at about 10 knots, a great whale appeared alongside and swam with us for about 15 hours. The great animal kept up her speed and was close alongside all the time. We were fortunate enough to have a sailor on board who had worked for many years on the great factory ships that worked in the Antarctic processing the whales that were caught by the smaller whale catchers. This sailor was a Norwegian and held a Master Mariner's Certificate in steam and sail, he explained that the whale was a "killer" whale or "grampus", and that it had probably been injured in a fight and his wounds were bleeding, so he was keeping close to the tanker to get away from the rest of the pack who would challenge him for his place in the pack, possibly as leader. He also told us that the smell of the tanker would disguise the smell of the blood and the whale could get away from the vicinity of the other whales, until his wounds were healed.

On another occasion we were loading a full cargo of 18,000 tons of aviation spirit, at a small refinery called the Orange Refinery in Texas, in the River Neches and the cargo was destined for the United Kingdom. The spirit was coming aboard at about 800 tons per hour and we were kept busy filling the various tanks.

The Captain and the Radio Officer had gone ashore to attend the Naval Routing Office during the morning and were due back very soon. The tugs and pilot arrived alongside at 1600 hrs and we all knew our sailing time was very close at hand, but the Captain and Sparks were not yet back from the Convoy Conference.

At 1650 the Captain and the Radio Officer returned to the ship and we sailed outwards for the United Kingdom. Everything went off in a normal manner and the vessel sailed at 1900 hrs, proceeded down the river and out into the Gulf of Mexico.

Three tankers left the river within a few minutes of each other and set their courses as instructed by the United States Naval Instructions. As soon as we were clear of the river we were instructed to open envelope "Y" and obey its orders. On opening envelope "Y" we were instructed to proceed to a certain position where we would reach a buoy marked "No.1" which was given also in latitude and longitude. The course necessary to make this position was given, and we were due to arrive at the buoy at 0100 hrs the next morning.

I had read the naval instructions myself, so you can imagine how surprised I was to hear the Captain order an entirely different course, in fact a course that would take us some 60 miles South into the Gulf of Mexico and well away from the coast. When I quietly questioned the Captain on this unusual action, his answer to me was straight and to the point. He said "God knows who has had access to these orders." He felt that there were far too many Germans of American birth in the U.S.A. He, the Captain, thought that the less people ashore knew of our whereabouts the better it would be for all.

At 0106 hrs the next morning the Radio Officer received a message from the other tankers, saying they had been torpedoed, were on fire and sinking. By this time we were too far away to reach them. My ship had an uneventful passage to Key West where we formed a coastal convoy with U.S.A. naval vessels as our escorts and planes and airships keeping watch overhead, until we reached our destination, New York.

There comes a time when Ship's Masters find themselves entirely on their own, and decisions that can only be intuitive have to be taken as a calculated risk, and if they prove to be right then they pay off to the advantage of all concerned. As they said in those days "Careless Talk Costs Lives" and I am afraid that saying was very true. One could never tell who had access to very confidential papers. It was best to assume that the papers had been seen by the wrong people and work accordingly, to be safe.

Inside the Arctic Circle, 1941

59

Chapter 6

On one occasion during the war, we were sent on a very unusual voyage. The Captain and the Radio Officer had returned from the Convoy Conference in Avonmouth at about 1640 hrs and I noticed, as the Captain came up the gangway that he looked a little put out, and without a word to anyone went up the bridge ladder to his cabin. I, being Chief Officer of the ship, was busy attending to our final ballasting arrangements before sailing and was out on deck, when the Captain's steward came and informed me, with the Captain's compliments, that he would like to see me in his cabin as soon as possible.

I went up to the Captain's cabin and knocked on the dayroom door, a moment later a voice from within sang out "Come in No. 1." I entered the cabin and found the Captain sitting on his settee sorting out some papers from his briefcase. "Sit down No. 1, I have one or two things to enlighten you upon." he said. "First, we haven't received the usual passage information from the convoy Commodore and have no destination for this coming voyage. It would seem that we are proceeding outwards under sealed orders and all we know is that we call at New York for further orders, after that we have no knowledge whatsoever of our future. All we have been told is to keep well topped up with bunkers, stores and fresh water, so please see we are well equipped in all respects for a long voyage."

We finally sailed from Avonmouth in the Bristol Channel in single line ahead convoy for Belfast in Northern Ireland, where we joined an ocean convoy which was gathering together for the main convoy for New York. Our instructions were to weigh anchor at 0115 hrs, and be ready to steam outwards through the boom defence at 0145 hrs. This we did and proceeded towards the Western Approaches in double line ahead.

North of Ratlin, on the north coast of Northern Ireland, we formed the convoy into its proper block formation and the Escort Vessels took up their screening positions. Planes of Coastal Command were busy overhead, and were making wide sweeps over the whole area to the westwards, on the look-out for enemy submarines and planes. Once formed up the convoy commenced zig-zagging towards the United States of America.

Various convoy orders from the Commodore were passed by flag or Aldis lamp through the afternoon and all preparations for the long, dark night were made during the hours of daylight. The night passed without further trouble until the first light at the break of dawn, when four German planes attacked the convoy from the north. They came in fairly low and crossed the convoy from north to south. Fourteen bombs were dropped but no direct hits were made, but one of the leading bombers was hit right on the nose by a shell from the 12 lb, 12 cwt., anti-aircraft gun on the Shell Mex tanker the s.s. "Drupa". The plane came down in a long slow glide, with volumes of smoke coming from the main body of the plane and was last seen passing out of sight, just above the water to the West North West. Apart from running into dense fog for about five days and nights the rest of the passage was uneventful and we all finally reached New York, and were all allotted an anchorage in the area known as Man-O-War Anchorage, in the great harbour.

After attending the U.S. Naval Conference in New York City, all the ships that were proceeding further afield left New

York and proceeded out to sea in single file, keeping well into the shore and using the Chesapeaks and Delaware Canals on our voyage South to the Florida Straits and the Gulf of Mexico. We finally arrived at the port of Corpus Christi in Texas and there we loaded a full cargo of 17,800 tons of high grade fighter spirit destined for we knew not where.

After leaving Corpus Christi we proceeded out of the Gulf of Mexico and at a certain position opened envelope No.2, which instructed us to proceed through the Panama Canal to Panama City and store ship, take fresh water and proceed to a position south of the Galapagos Islands then south down the Pacific Ocean, zig-zagging all the time and therefore covering great distances. We carried on around Cape Horn, across the South Atlantic Ocean, close to the Falkland Islands, onto South Georgia to a position 300 miles south of Capetown. We were then instructed to sail into Capetown and store ship and take fuel and fresh water. We were in Capetown for about 36 hrs and then left. On leaving Capetown we again sailed for the same spot on the chart 300 miles south and altered our course to the N.N. East and out into the Indian Ocean.

After some days sailing N.N. East we altered course to a N.N. Westerly direction towards the Gulf of Aden and through the Red Sea to Port Said, where we finally discharged our cargo of fighter spirit.

Three vessels had been chosen for this priority job as the R.A.F. were in dangerously short supply and the government of the day decided to send three ships independently and unescorted, so as to draw as little attention to themselves as possible and I'm pleased to say that all three of us reached our destination safely, and the Royal Air Force received a large surplus of spirit for their planes, much to the satisfaction of all concerned.

The voyage was a very long one and owing to the short days, very tedious and dangerous to boot, as we could have been torpedoed or sunk by surface craft, and could have expected no help of any sort. We were unescorted and many miles from normal shipping lanes. We could have been attacked and sunk without trace if we had been torpedoed in a vital part of our structure. The cargo, being high grade fighter spirit, would have gone off like a plumber's blow lamp with no chance of survival or rescue. As we had to zig-zag all the way, I believe we covered somewhere in the region of 32,000 miles on this memorable voyage.

Chapter 7

We had loaded a full cargo of aviation spirit in Bullen Bay in Curacao in the Dutch West Indies and were on our way home in a convoy of about forty ships of all sorts and sizes.

The voyage was uneventful until we were about eight days from the West coast of Ireland where we ran into dense fog with visibility of only a quarter of a mile or less.

The convoy of ships was well closed up in their positions and keeping close up to the fog buoys which were being trailed by the ship ahead and which was the only thing in sight for most of the time.

Our Captain was getting very worried about our real position because we had had no sights for several hours, in fact no true fix for about 60 hours or so and the South West coast of Ireland was coming closer all the time. Our direction finder was playing up and we couldn't get any reliable bearings from it. We had no spares and therefore could not effect a repair.

I was the 2nd Officer and therefore the Navigating Officer of the ship. It was now up to me to try to obtain the most accurate position possible and as soon as possible. I had noticed that there was a good bright moon by which, with good luck, I might get a decent horizon. I decided to leave the Navigation Bridge, which was about fifty-five feet above sea level, and come down to the main deck, which was about seven feet above sea level, and would give me a much nearer horizon and therefore a better and more accurate sextant sight. The position on the main deck was much better for the chance of a good sight and the horizon much clearer.

I sat on a wooden box for some long time between 0100hrs and 0400hrs during the Middle Watch and looked for a break in the mist that would help to to obtain a better view of the horizon.

Well, I took several sights of suitable stars and the moon for good luck and arrived at what I thought was the best position I could possibly get and placed my findings on the Atlantic chart and, much to my surprise, found that my postion was about fourteen miles North of the noon position as given by the Commodore of the convoy in the lead ship. I showed this position to the Captain of my ship and he said I must have made a mistake as he said all the other ships put the convoy fourteen to fifteen miles south. I checked my work several times, but always arrived at the same results.

Being satisfied that my calculations were correct and that the convoy was really much further North than we thought, I advised our Captain that he should be on the Bridge from 2130hrs onwards that night. His reaction was that I was "off my head", but I was pleased to see that he went up to the wheelhouse before 2130hrs and stayed there with the 3rd Officer.

At about 2240hrs a Green Very Light shot across the sky and the Captain shouted out "What is that?" I told the Captain that the signal meant "Alter course to starboard 45° to be obeyed when seen". The Captain gave the order to the quartermaster to alter course to starboard and, as the ship swung to starboard we saw the lighthouse on Galley Head on the South coast of Ireland swinging across our bows to port.

The lead ship of the Port Column ran high and dry on the rocks, her name if I remember correctly was "THE BOTHAVEN". We never did hear any more about her as there were very tight restrictions on keeping radio silence.

There must be some sort of record here, because I was the only one of about forty ships that had the correct position. The moon and my wooden box on the main deck had paid off.

Incidently, the following morning there was not one of

the forty ships to be seen, the next time we saw any of them was when we were off the Bar Lightship in the approaches to the River Mersey. They had really scattered after seeing that Green Very Light.

Cut Down to Size

Our Master was requested to call upon the N.O.I.C., ie. (Naval Officer In Command) at Scapa Flow at 1000hrs on a certain day.

At 0940hrs, on the day in question, the Captain arrived at the accommodation ladder resplendent in his No.1 winter uniform complete with kid gloves and a chest full of medal ribbons. The Captain was 6'4", tall and handsome to boot. He boarded the duty launch and was whisked ashore. He was taken across to the landing steps and shown where he could find the N.O.I.C. When he arrived at the wooden hut he was asked by the Blue Jacket on guard duty what he required. He told the guard what he wanted and was then taken into the hut where in a small room to the right he was announced and shown in.

The Blue Jacket told the Officer, who was sitting at a desk, that a gentleman wished to speak to him. The Officer sitting at the desk did not look up and for a full six minutes kept the Captain standing there. He then slowly put his pen down on the desk and looked up, he looked the Captain up and down two or three times and then said in a tired voice, "Who are you and what are you?"

The Captain laughed and said, "There hangs a tale. The Board of Trade call me the Master, my Company call me the Captain, my Crew call me the Skipper and my Wife calls me Bill. And you sonny can stand to attention, take your hands out of your pockets and call meSIR!"

Chapter 8

In August 1944 we sailed outward bound from Liverpool for Belfast in Northern Ireland, and in Belfast Lough we anchored with many other vessels of all types and sizes. We were all waiting for orders for forming up the main Ocean Convoy. After two or three days waiting we left Belfast in convoy for New York, U.S.A. In New York we were routed via the Straits of Florida to Houston, Texas in the Gulf of Mexico, where we loaded 10,000 tons of U.S. Navy fuel oil. We sailed from Houston under orders to Gantanamo Bay, Cuba, where we were instructed to proceed through the Panama Canal and across the Pacific Ocean to Sydney, Australia. During our transit of the Panama Canal we had about 16 American Marines placed on board our vessel to see that no person did anything to endanger the safe passage of the vessel through the Canal. We had two guards armed with machine guns, pointing them straight at us on the Fo'c's'le head, three guards on the bridge, four in the engine room and four in the general accommodation with two more on the Poop deck and an officer in charge of the lot. The four who patrolled the ship's accommodation also kept a strict watch on the steering flat and kept it locked most of the way through the Canal. They only opened the steering flat to see all was well and then locked it again, always leaving a guard nearby. We were Allies of the United States of America, but I am afraid they didn't trust us very far. Still, better safe than sorry.

On reaching the Panama City end of the Canal we saw a great commotion over near the shore, we found out later that there were some U.S. Marines swimming in the water near Balboa Town wharf and one of them had had his leg bitten off by a shark.

I sould mention here, that on our arrival in New York from Belfast we went into Brooklane Dry Dock and had a complete new accommodation house put into place onto the foundations that had been put in place in England. A crew of welders came on board and in a few hours had welded the new house onto our after boat deck. It was complete in every respect, it even had curtains at the portholes, lavatories in the correct places so that they just had to be connected up and all was in working order, within 24 hours. Thirty four D.E.M.S. personnel had moved in and one would have thought they had been there for ages. We also took on board twelve Maritime Ack Ack Regiment members who occupied the house on the port side of our boat deck which had been constructed some months before. All these men stayed with us for the whole length of the Pacific Campaign, and they were fine chaps every one. They were discharged in Bombay, India, in February 1946, I believe it was. About four of the D.E.M.S. ratings stayed with us and were discharged in Swansea in April 1946, when our ship returned to England after that long and epic voyage.

When we arrived in Sydney for the first time, we were one of the very first vessels of the British Pacific Fleet Train to arrive in these Australian Waters, and the Australian Authorities didn't know what to do with us, so we spent some time carrying fuel oil around the coast to places such as Brisbane, Newcastle, Cairns, Darwin, Adelaide, Port Pirrie and Port Lincoln from the oil depot in Sydney. We were lavishly entertained by the various Australian families who wanted to show some effort towards the British Merchant men who were there to fight the war. Their hospitality was of the essence and

The author in Sydney, Australia 1945,
at the end of the war, aged 35 years.
Chief Officer of the m.v. "San Adolfo"

very generous to us all. I shall never forget those wonderful people.

On a Sunday morning sometime later when we were anchored in Sydney Harbour, the British Pacific Fleet Train arrived and sailed into the harbour. They came through the Sydney Heads in a never ending stream a sight never to be forgotten, and certainly never to be seen again. There were Battleships, Cruisers, Aircraft Carriers, Destroyers, Corvettes, Frigates and Submarines and all their attendant craft. Never in the annals of history had Sydney or anywhere else for that matter, seen such a magnificent sight. Some time later all the Commanders and Captains of all the ships were called aboard the Battleship H.M.S. "King George V" for a conference with their Commanding Officer Admiral Archer, funny to say, the same name as the Master of my ship, Captain Archer who, from the day they were introduced thence forward called each other "Namesake".

The prime matter to be considered at the conference was the exercise to be carried out between the Battleship and my ship, the m.v. "San Adolfo" at sea at our full speed of 12/13 knots. We were to go out to sea with the Battleship H.M.S. "King George V" and perform an Oiling At Sea Exercise. The exercise turned out to be a huge failure, and was called off.

When my Captain came back from the conference on the Battleship, he told me what had been planned for the coming exercise. On the day in question we sailed out to the arranged exercise area and closed up alongside the Battleship, at our full speed of 13 knots. A marker line was passed across forward, it was marked at six foot intervals by a small piece of red bunting, and each end was held by hand by a rating on each ship. They held the marker line taut all the time and this helped the two ships to keep their distance from each other. We then received a thin "Costain Gun Line" from the K.G.V. which was attached to a two and a half inch Sisal rope which was in turn made fast to a 15" three stranded triple cable laid hawser. When all was ready, my twelve sailors commenced hauling all these ropes aboard and flaking them down along our fore deck. When all was inboard, a messenger (i.e. a light line) was sent across from the K.G.V. and made fast to the 15" hawser. A signal was given to the Battleship and about 200 blue jackets commenced to heave the hawser across to their ship. My 12 able seamen on board the tanker commenced to heave the hawser out through the lead and all went well until the bight of the hawser got down into the water, then it started to take charge. My men couldn't hold it so had to let go and jump clear. The 200 men on the Battleship held on tightly until the Sisal messenger snapped and they all fell backwards with the soles of 400 feet facing up to the sky! The 15" hawser now free, ran out of my ship like a great snake, fortunately I had taken the precaution of putting the eye of the hawser over the bits and when the end came it pulled up with a jerk and trailed down the ships' side, our only danger now was the rope getting into the propeller.

I sent instructions to the bridge to start turning slowly to port until we could retrieve the hawser and get it back on board. This we did, it was a very difficult job bringing in 900 feet of 15" rope in small fleets. Nevertheless we got sufficient hawser inboard to enable us to get a couple of turns on to the barrel of the windlass, we were able to haul all the remaining rope out of the water and clear of our propeller. There was no serious damage but the exercise was never attempted again. The whole exercise was a complete fiasco and was abandoned. Oiling At Sea was henceforth carried out with only the marker line across between the two ships. The whole idea was to pass the heavy line across to the Battleship to form a bridle on which she could keep a steady fixed station on the vessel doing the oiling and storing, in this case the oiler was my ship the m.v. "San Adolfo".

Many thousands of tons of fuel oil was given to the ships of the fleet, at our full speed of about 13 knots and all fuellings were very successful and carried out in the shortest possible time, mostly without damage of any sort. Only one destroyer whose Captain seemed a little nervous when so close alongside, fell back on his station and pulled all our oiling equipment into the sea. The big sixty foot long derricks came down with all the gear, such as topping lifts, saddle hose carriers and 5" hoses of which there were two. The lot came down smashing the ships' rails and bending the derricks almost double. All further oiling at sea had to stop until repairs could be carried out and new derricks obtained from Sydney.

On one occasion when we were refuelling the battleship H.M.S. "Howe" she fell back on station astern of us and pulled all our oiling gear into the sea. She lay there with two oiling hoses dangling from her bows, one hose was 1200 feet in length and the other, the short hose, was 1140 feet long, both hoses were attached to a two and a half inch circumference steel wire cable. The whole of our oiling gear was now dangling from the bows of the battleship and was a serious and dangerous embarrassment to her in enemy waters, the Captain gave orders for the cable to be cut with oxyacetylene torches. Ratings with these torches cut through the cable and sent all our gear, precious as it was, to the bottom of the Pacific Ocean. We received a signal from the Captain of the battleship H.M.S. "Howe" saying "So sorry San Adolfo but we have had to cut all your gear free. Please be ready for oiling at first light. Message ends." As all this took place at the end of the day, all my ratings, engineers and pump men and myself worked all night mostly in total darkness, to break out new gear and connect it

*H.M.S. "SWIFTSURE" fuelling on our Port Side,
Pacific Ocean 1944*

*H.M.S. "HOWE" Battleship fuelling over the stern,
Pacific Ocean 1944*

all up ready for oiling the fleet at dawn. The whole ship was covered in fuel oil, this occurred when the hoses were pulled out of the ship, and before we could stop our pumps in time. I am pleased to say that after a long hard night working under great difficulty we were ready as requested, for oiling the ships at 0630 hrs the following day. Owing to the danger of planes and Japanese submarines we were unable to use torches or lights of any sort during the hours of darkness, so natural night darkness had to do. When one has been working under these conditions for some time it is surprising what can be seen.

Most of the station keeping was of the highest standard and the various Captains had it all off to a fine art and showed pride in keeping station in the proper manner. They were very quick in connecting up their hoses and also very quick at disconnecting them. They kept their vessels steady on the oiling marks which were displayed on our ship for all to see. From passing the heavy line to commencing pumping, was done in four and a half minutes by the No. 1 and his crew on the destroyer H.M.S. "Undine". This was the record and he held it all the time we were in the Pacific. During those long gone days I had the pleasure of fuelling H.M.S. "Whelp", the ship on which Prince Phillip, the Duke of Edinburgh, was serving as No. 1. We fuelled her three times in 1945 giving her 50 tons on the first oiling, 257 tons on the second oiling and 260 tons on the third oiling.

On one occasion when H.M.S. "Swiftsure" the cruiser was dangerously short of fuel, the weather was so foul that she couldn't come alongside so we carried out her fuelling in a novel way. The "Swiftsure" anchored near one of the nearby islands and there was a very heavy swell running at the time, so we took up station some 600 feet ahead of her and dropped our port anchor. When we had brought up, we then paid out our anchor cable until we were close enough for safety and fired a Costain Gun Line across so that our hoses could be passed over to the cruiser. As soon as the hoses were connected up we commenced fuelling as if we were steaming along at sea in the usual oiling manner. Needless to say we received a really big pat on the back from the happy Captain of H.M.S. "Swiftsure" who had been getting very anxious about his bunker position. We also felt very happy that we were able to assist.

We became based on the island of Manus in the Admiralty Group of Islands, which lie north of New Guinea in the Bismark Sea, from here we gave the whole of the British Pacific Fleet all their worldly needs. We had on board our ship potatoes, turnips, carrots, cabbages, parsnips, flour and tinned food of every sort of brand, fresh water, whisky, gin, rum, beer, beef, mutton, pork, poultry and all types of household goods for cleaning the ship and its accommodation. Our aim was to be able to give them anything they might ask for by one of His Majesty's ships at war and many miles from her home port and serving in foreign places.

We carried small arms and ammunition of different calibre. We also carried about 60 depth charges, on the main deck under the amidships accommodation. Barrage balloons and the gas to inflate them was also available if wanted. We carried over 200 survivor kits, each set consisting of a warm jersey, trousers, vest and underpants, razor, soap, toothpaste and brush, a packet of razor blades and shoes of some sort. So one can see that we were of the greatest importance to the vessels of the Fleet as we carried without doubt, their life's blood. Fuel oil, hundreds of drums of lubricating oil were carried in our huge forward cargo hold and this was passed across on overhead lines to the various ships and craft that requested or had need for it. The fuel was passed across by pumping through 5" flexible rubber hoses, we always used two hoses at a time side by side, these were suspended from a derrick which carried a special curved saddle from which the hoses were suspended. All other types of stores were passed across to the ships needing them, on a wire set up between the two vessels and tended at each end by D.E.M.S. (Defensively Equipped Merchant Ships) ratings and Maritime Ack Ack soldiers on the ship and the operation worked very well throughout the whole length of the Pacific War.

We had a great many friends among the small attendant craft of the U.S. Fleet, and helped them as much as we could. Various American Fleet tugs, motor boats and other small craft did many useful jobs for us, and in turn we gave them petrol, lube oil and anything else we could spare. They in their turn saw we got fresh fruit, olives, clothing and many film picture shows etc. and many good friends were made by all.

There was no shortage of equipment and stores etc. in the Pacific because there was an almost continuous stream of vessels from the U.S.A. which kept up an uninterrupted supply of all that could possibly be needed, by warships and their attendant craft off station and away from their homeland during war time.

Our oiling equipment officer was one named Lt. Commander Venning and I am sure that without him the war in the Pacific would have ground to a full stop. How that wonderful chap kept us supplied with oiling gear and particularly rubber oiling hoses, I'll never know. Everyone was on his back asking for this and that and somehow he never failed to comply. He was the one officer who stuck in my mind from all the many dozens I had to deal with during the Pacific Campaign. He was an unselfish, hard working beaver of a chap and if ever anyone was to be honoured for his war work, then he should have been knighted. Without Lt. Commander Venning I hate to think what would have happened to us all, no hoses, no oil, no war of that I am sure.

Life has some very funny angles at times. My ship was the first vessel of the British Pacific Fleet Train to arrive out in Australia and the Pacific waters. We stayed there for 23 months and served the fleet vessels continuously, but we never had a mention of any sort nor were we or our crew honoured in any way.

All the Admiralty forms required for recommendation were filled in by Captain H.C. Archer and sent to the proper authorities but we never even received a note of thanks to the Ship's Company, saying "Well done San Adolfo". All the other ships which only served for a few weeks, were well decorated and various awards for their efforts, were received from the authorities. I have always felt sorry about this, because I did hope that my wife and my mother might have had the pleasure of seeing the King close up at the investiture, but it was not to be.

Several of my friends who only spent about three months out in the Pacific received the O.B.E. but we who served for $22^1/2$ months received nothing. This of course was the luck of the draw in wartime. The more one did the less one was thought of.

I mentioned before that we had a continuous supply of war materials which were being shipped from the western ports of the U.S.A. to keep us going, it was like an endless belt and all the necessary supplies kept coming.

When the U.S. Army Air Force left an area of incident, they just stood up and left on command taking only their personal possessions with them. They marched out and their camps were left just as they were, almost intact. Soon there was a public outcry from the people of Australia, wanting to know why the U.S. Army Air Force were leaving war equipment all over the islands of the Pacific and at last, one day came the official answer. A U.S. Army Colonel came onto the Australian Broadcasting Network and said "People here in Australia are asking why the U.S. Army Forces are leaving war equipment all over the islands of the Pacific and I have been given the job of explaining and giving them an answer, so here it is. Why shift a goddam junk heap, from one place to somewhere else." What the public did not know or understand was, that if the equipment in question which was being left on the various beaches, was collected and taken to the next area of combat, then thousands of men and many ships would have to be taken off their other vital duties to handle this equipment, and the steady flow of war materials from the U.S.A. factories would be disrupted and a smooth flow of supplies upset. So it was better by far to leave everything except each man's own equipment behind than to take it to the next area of combat, which was sure to have plenty of everything supplied from existing U.S.A. sources.

On one occasion I landed with a boat crew on one of the islands near Manus. We met the head man of the village and his retinue. As we approached the island we could see that almost all the women were naked, and as we approached closer to the shore they all ran into their huts and came out a moment or so later wearing European dresses. The small boys of the village climbed up the coconut palms and knocked down nuts for us to take back to the ship, they knocked down about 20 nuts in a few minutes.

After our introduction to the head man by a young man of about 18 years of age, who could speak a few words of English, we made the boat well fast to some large palms and went off into what had once been a great coconut plantation, it had once been well cultivated but was now neglected. Several hundred trees went to make up this plantation. After some good walking we came across a deserted U.S. Army camp, the huts stood just as they had been left. My crew loaded themselves with everything one could think of in the way of household equipment, there was plenty of cutlery, folding chairs all stamped with the U.S.A. stamp. My Bo'sun asked me if he could take the harmonium from the little church for use on board our ship and I agreed. They took from the camp some brushes, dustpans, paint brushes and various pieces of wearing apparel. My crew used the harmonium for the remainder of the voyage and some very good music and singsongs were enjoyed in the evenings.

On some occasions we saw huge 16,000 ton American Army supply vessels loaded right up to the level of the navigation bridge structure, and all its holds packed tight with equipment of every kind that one can think of. There were complete ambulances, with all their surgical equipment for handling seriously injured and wounded men, jeeps, radio and radar equipment, electrical equipment, dynamos, electric motors and many other things one could name. These ships were taken out to sea, not too far from Manus Harbour by a skeleton crew and a couple of large holes were cut in the sides of the ship, by the engineers who had gone out with the ship, in order to take the skeleton crew back to base. The ship slowly sank in very deep water, this was just to get rid of surplus and unwanted materials and to make room for new supplies which were coming in all the time in one continuous stream.

My crew took a large 16 cu.ft. refrigerator of the domestic type off one of these ships before it was disposed of and they fixed it up in the crew's quarters in their messroom and ran it for the rest of the voyage. We were able to get almost anything we required from the Americans, they had more of everything than they could possibly use. We were also given free medical and dental treatment whenever it was necessary. On one occasion I was asked if there was anything I required, by two U.S. Naval Officers, and I told them that I would like to have a pair of their lovely Officer's khaki silk finish uniform trousers and a shirt to match. They took my measurements and the next day sent me 12 shirts and 12 pairs of trousers, from then onwards I was the best dressed officer in the Pacific.

We used to work off the coast of Japan for several weeks then we would return back down south to Manus for a rest and clean up ship. The destroyers always liked to tie up alongside our ship, so that they could let go easily and make a quick get away in the event of an emergency. We used to have two destroyers made fast on each side of our ship, we had our two anchors down, and the warships tied up on each side. We were entertained by the Royal Naval Officers in their wardrooms and of course we returned the compliment. In the evening we watched good film shows, out on deck in the warmth of the tropical night. The screens were set up on the warship's deck and we all sat on forms in the balmy warm night air and enjoyed very good entertainment.

After a week to ten day's rest and cleaning ship we again left Manus and proceeded North to the fuelling area and resumed fuelling the warships off Japan. We were attacked from the air a couple of times but there were no casualties, our greatest trouble was floating mines which the Japs dropped in the oiling area during the night. The water was too deep to anchor the mines hence the reason for using floating mines, they no doubt hoped we would run into them during the night and suffer severe damage or maybe sink. I think the displacement wash from our ships must just have pushed the floating mines aside as we passed by, for no ship ever struck one of these mines to my knowledge, during the time we operated in the Pacific oiling area. Japanese planes came out and looked at us from time to time, but we were never really troubled by them. We fuelled our warships about 160 times, at our full speed of 13 knots and gave them all their needs to do the job of fighting the Japs. The lads of the Pacific Fleet Train were the finest in the world and great chaps to work with and I include all the Europeans and Americans in this statement. A fine spirit of friendship grew up between the men of the Merchant Navy and those of the Royal Navy, both grew to respect the work which was done by the other and they realised they were all part of a great team. We had a common job to do and everyone played his or her part to the full. Sleep and rest were grabbed where and when possible, a three hour sleep was considered an all night in bed session and everyone rested when they could.

There were no back sliders and everyone worked round the clock twice on many occasions, all without a grumble. Food was often taken in one's hand, in large sandwich form, with steaming mugs of tea or coffee to wash it down. One couldn't leave the job for a moment, there was no time to sit in messrooms and take a meal in the usual fashion when we were oiling ships of the fleet. Everyone was busy tending to the warships and seeing to the various needs.

The Captain and Officers of my ship the m.v "San Adolfo" were entertained on several occasions on board the battleships and aircraft carriers and a fine and jolly time was had by all. This was usually done when we were fuelling the various ships in the port of Manus or Sydney, these were the periods when we had more time to relax. We then had more time to enjoy these get togethers and with everyone more rested and relaxed we had a good time and were able to get to know each other better. It was a very unusual feeling to leave a battleship after a very enjoyable evening at about 2230 hrs and be asked to stand on a large flat tray, which was normally used for lifting cargoes, and be hoisted high into the dark night sky, with all the Naval Officers, who had so recently been our hosts, all standing to attention and saluting us as we were swung clear of their deck and carefully lowered down onto the deck of our own ship which was usually moored alongside, nevertheless a good safe way of transferring personnel from one ship to another. On two or three occasions we had the good fortune to be invited on board American tankers for a meal. They were fresh out from the United States and had loads of fresh food aboard. They gave us huge steaks, loads of ice cream and also fresh fruit and cream, food we hadn't seen for months except on one or two very special occasions.

We worked in an oiling area of about 300 miles east to west and 150 miles north to south. The north-west corner of the oiling area was about 145 miles from Tokyo. We steamed around this area all the time and as we emptied out our fuel oil, so we were reloaded by a fleet of U.S. tankers which kept coming from the U.S.A. Western Seaboard all the time. They kept up a steady supply of fuel and stores to the American and British oiling fleets. As this operation was carried out at our full speed of about 13 knots the only way we could decide we had received enough fuel oil from the American tanker supply vessels was when the toilets on the deck above the tonnage deck would not flush. We then knew we could not take any more oil on board and remain safe from a stability point of view. In wartime and under duress one did things that would never be allowed in peace time.

On some occasions when we were fuelling the battleships and cruisers I was knocked over by the heavy seas which were passing between the two vessels at a speed of 12 to 13 knots. Now and again the sea would break over the decks and as I had to keep on deck to look after the job of oiling I would be inundated, washed off my feet and hurled along the deck until I came up to the surface against the accommodation bulkhead at the after end of the main deck. I surfaced to loud cheers of hundreds of blue jackets on the decks of the battleships or cruisers. I am pleased to be able to report that I was never hurt in any way but always got a good soaking and the odd bruise here and there and my dignity somewhat dented.

The only real hurt that I sustained was to my eyes. During an oiling operation one has to watch the derricks and saddles which carry the oiling hoses for any signs of excessive tension coming on the gear, otherwise it would part and all come down on the deck causing much delay. After oiling on a very bright day, I found on going to my cabin at about 1700 hrs after finishing the days oiling of several ships, that I couldn't see. Both my eyes were heavily blistered from the sun, and it never really manifested itself until I went into the darkened interior of the accommodation. I had to stay in my cabin resting for several days, having my eyes bathed at frequent intervals with something sent over from the Surgeon Commander on H.M.S. "King George V". After about six days my eyes were much better and after ten days they were normal once again. The blisters just dried up and went back on the surface of the eye ball and although the surface appeared to be a bit rough and rippled for a while, it never seemed to give me any trouble. I'm now 81 years of age and my sight is just normal for my age, I wear glasses for reading and driving, but can still see very well without glasses of any sort.

We had many friends among the small craft of the American Fleet and they looked after us very well in many ways. There was always a tug or a small seagoing launch available if we required one, and in return we kept them topped up with petrol and diesel oil for their engines, and of course they were always welcome to the odd can of beer or a little dram of the hard stuff if they so desired. As all American ships were quite dry as far as intoxicating drink was concerned, you can imagine how well we were patronised. They were good well behaved chaps and became good friends, what a pity we have long since lost touch.

On one occasion I happened to say that I liked olives. Two days later a launch arrived alongside with a consignment of olives for No.1 i.e. me, the Chief Officer. At least that's what the able seaman who brought them on board said. I went down to the main deck to receive the packet of olives from the rating and you can imagine my surprise when I found that he had brought me two five gallon drums of olives, one drum large green olives and the other drum was of the larger black olives. Needless to say we never ran out of olives during our time in the Pacific Ocean. Not many of the crew liked them very much, but those who did had a good feed of lovely fresh olives.

On our occasional trips to Sydney, for a rest and clean up ship, that is, fresh coat of paint all round and a new supply of stores for ourselves and also replenishing stores for the warships and their attendant craft. During our stay in Sydney we were lavishly entertained by the "Shell Mex Company" of Sydney, and also by various families who made it their business to come to our ship and introduce themselves. The Mission to Seamen were mostly responsible for this, and all our ratings and all the officers were invited to the various people's homes as guests and given a very enjoyable time. We also returned the compliment and gave several parties for the families on board our ship which were very well enjoyed by all who attended.

One evening I was visited by the priest from the Mission to Seamen, who said he had some bad news for me and proceeded to tell me how he had found my Bo'sun Mr. Carl Olin hanged in the ventilation well of the Mission to Seamen building. No one ever realised that there was anything the matter with the Bo'sun, and this was a terrible shock to us all. The Bo'sun was a company man of long standing and was well liked by us all. He was a Russian by birth but had lived in the north of England for many years. No one ever suspected that he would ever take his own life, we were all devastated by this horrible calamity. We had the Bo'sun buried in Botany Bay Cemetery and most of the ship's company attended the funeral.

We had one other death on board the ship and that was the senior pumpman Mr. J. Kelly who died of natural causes whilst we were at sea, on our way from Manus to Sydney with various units of the fleet. The pumpman was buried at sea at 1600 hrs. The Ensign on our ship was lowered to the half-mast position, and all the other vessels in the fleet followed suit, all stopping their engines at the same time. The burial service was read by the Captain of our ship, Captain H.C. Archer, the body was committed to the deep at 1615 hrs. Ensigns were drawn close up, all engines put to full speed and the convoy resumed its passage to Australia. It was a very funny thing that the weather had been lovely and sunny, but as it approached 1600 hrs the sky became very dark and threatening and at 1615 hrs the sun came out and once again it became a lovely day. Someone seemed to be watching overhead!

One of our last oiling jobs was in Subic Bay in Luzon in the Philippines and we were at anchor when we received the message from the Admiralty that the war with Japan was at last over, that was on the 3rd September 1945. All the vessels, many different types of British and American fleets let off flares, smoke bombs, and tracer ammunition by way of celebration. It had been a long hard war and we were glad to be alive to see its end. Many good friends never lived to see this great day, when Germany and Japan were beaten to their knees but they will never be forgotten, even to this day 46 years later one still remembers them as they were in their prime. Fine strong patriotic young men of sterling character.

My ship the m.v. "San Adolfo" was about the first ship of the British Pacific Fleet Train to arrive out in Pacific waters and one of the last to leave after the war ended. I have always been sorry that we never received any recognition for our long hard task of keeping the many vessels of the fleet train supplied with their fuel oil, lubricating oils, and all stores needed to keep a war ship at sea and in top fighting condition while many miles away from their home station. We fuelled these vessels for 22$^1/2$ months, yet tankers who only spent a few weeks fuelling the fleet returned home and received decorations and commendations for their work but my ship never received any decoration or recognition of any kind. As far as I am concerned I would have awarded my crew medals as big as churches for the work they did, without a murmur of any kind, all the hours of the day and night. They were all good Tynesiders and patriots to a man. Every man that joined the ship at the commencement of the voyage, with the exception of two who died, and two, that I as Chief Officer had sacked as undesirables, paid off the ship in Swansea in April 1946 on our arrival home.

I'm glad to say that most of my friends in other ships did receive recognition and were given the O.B.E. and other decorations according to their rank, for services rendered. We for some reason, unknown to us, were never recognised or ever given credit at all. I was very sorry about this, not that I cared for myself, but I was concerned for our crew. I also hoped that if I received a decoration, then my Mother and my Wife would have been able to see the King at very close quarters. I have always regretted not seeing King George VI face to face.

My ship was instrumental in giving the British Pacific Fleet about 160,000 tons of fuel oil and vast quantities of stores of every description and my crew worked like slaves day and night, there was never a grumble nor yet a glum face throughout the whole of the long and hard campaign.

I had 33 D.E.M.S. naval ratings under Chief Petty Officer Cooper who had fought the German's great battleship "Admiral Graf Spey" in the battle of the River Plate in South America. I also had 11 Maritime Ack Ack under Sergeant Minchen ex Desert Rats. These men formed the actual defence of our vessel and helped me whenever and wherever required in the maintenance of the ship during the whole of the campaign. Both Chief Petty Officer Cooper and Sergeant Minchen were recovering from wounds, so they were sent to us with the hope that they would get more rest than in a warship. I am pleased to say they left the ship in Bombay in the pink of good health.

Morning, noon and night were all the same to our ship's company, they had come to do a job and nothing was going to stop them or stand in their way. They were great chaps, all of them, and should have been decorated for their devotion to duty, under very trying and difficult times. I wonder now, 47 years later, how many of these sterling fellows are still in the land of the living. Most of them were a few years younger than me and I am now just 81 years of age, so I am sure some of them are still living up on the Tyne.

We didn't return home immediately after the war, but carried several cargoes from Abadan to such places as Bombay, Karachi and Port Said. We loaded a full cargo of fuel oil in Abadan and took it via Suez where we shipped several passengers from Port Said, who were returning home to England. Brigadier General Thornhill and his lovely wife Dame Rachel Thornhill, the two most important people in the party, they had served for many years in the court of the Russian Czar and were members of the Diplomatic Service. The other passengers were employees of "Shell Mex" going home on leave, both men and women.

Perhaps here would be a good place to tell a few stories that might be of interest to the reader.

On arrival in Manus Island one of the first people we came in contact with was a huge man, who was an American Beachmaster, these were the chaps who were the first to land on the island and examine the territory and preparing the place for the troops when they landed. A huge provisions store was the first to go up, then a couple of churches, a medical centre and a dentist's office with about six dental chairs in a row. Dental experts were there to attend anyone who needed treatment, no matter who they were. I, myself, had two teeth filled at no cost by an expert dentist. We were able to buy cigarettes and tobacco, sweets, clothing and every other thing one wanted, all at very low cost.

One of the most baffling things that the Pacific Islands army forces came up against was the way the Japanese soldiers could kill American and Australian soldiers in what seemed to be total darkness in the tropical jungle. They never made the mistake of killing or harming their own men and this became a great mystery to the Allied Command. After one of the battles late in the war, the Japanese suffered a great defeat and many of their troops were killed, the American Officer in charge gave orders for the bodies of the Japanese dead to be collected up and made into a suitable pile for mass cremation. Camp guards were told off to look at the pile during the night, to see no animals desecrated the bodies.

It was somewhere about midnight when the first sentry went along the jungle path to the clearing which contained the dead corpses and the sight that met his eyes, frightened the life out of him. The whole mass of bodies was glowing with a blue and shimmering light in the night blackness. The sentry ran back to the camp and alerted his commanding officer telling him what he had seen. A full investigation was carried out and the great problem was solved. It was well known that most Japanese soldiers carried a small glass bottle on their belts, which everyone took to be a bottle of drinking water. This in fact, was not so, it was found on close inspection that these bottles contained fireflies. So you see any fireflies that moved about in the jungle at night was either a real firefly or another Japanese soldier, any other dark object moving in the jungle at night could only be an American or Australian soldier and must be stalked quietly and killed.

Here is a list of the vessels of the "Royal Navy" that I fuelled during the Pacific Campaign over a period of 22$^{1}/_{2}$ months.

Battleships:	Howe	**Cruisers:**	Swiftsure
	King George V		Argonaut
			Black Prince
Aircraft	Formidable		Euralus
Carriers:	Chaser		Newfoundland
	Ruler		Uganda
			Achilles
Destroyers:	Quilliam		Gambia
	Quickmatch		Areadne*
	Grenville		Undine
	Quiberon		Queenborough
	Urania		Whelp
	Urchin		Undaunted
	Wessex		Ulster
	Whirlwind		Kempenfelt
	Norman		Ursa
	Nepal		Nizam
	Napier		Teaser
	Barfleur		Ulysses
	Quadrant		Termigant
	Quality		Wizard
			Wakeful
Mine	Whyalla	**Frigates:**	Avon
Sweepers:	Ballarat		Whimbril
	Bendigo		Parrott
	Launceston		Usk
	Lismore		
	Pirie	**Sloops:**	Findhorn
	Gawler		Pheasant
	Geraldton		Redpole
	Burnie		Ipswich

* (Mine layer)

Many other small craft were fuelled including many American small craft. In all we gave the fleet and its attendant craft somewhere in the region of 160,000 tons of Navy Type Fuel Oil.

One evening when in Manus on anchor watch I received a message in morse code from the shore station to say, "Regret to inform you that Able Seaman Mr. X's Father has died." The next night about the same time I again received a message in morse code saying, "Please inform Mr. X Second Steward that his Father has died." On the third night I again received a message saying, "Please inform Chief Officer Mr. J. D. Nash that his Father has died." It was very unusual to receive three messages or signals as they were called, one night after the other and then to personally take the message myself and read it letter by letter and slowly realise it was my own Dad who was dead.

Owing to strict censorship we were very much out of touch with our families during this campaign. All we received was a mostly blacked out card type of letter saying, "Dear John", and one or two rather unimportant sentences followed by - "Love Edith." My Wife received the same kind of letters, so we were really out of touch most of the time over the two years.

Chapter 9

When I met my wife on the dockside in Swansea, in April 1946, we shook hands first and after some few long seconds with our arms round each other we timidly kissed, not really knowing how to behave. Of course this shyness soon passed off and we picked up the threads of our affection and love for each other. A few nights loving attention brought us back to our true and loving state. We never wanted to be parted again from each other and soon made up our minds to seek a change.

After about 4¹/₂ weeks leave I was sent off once more on an 11 month voyage. I am pleased to say that this voyage was curtailed and we were called back home to the United Kingdom for fresh orders. I did a few more voyages of short duration, seven weeks or thereabout and was promoted to Master of a vessel called the m.v. "San Ambrosio", a tanker of some 13,000 tons burden. On returning home to England I was relieved by a chum of mine and instructed to take three weeks leave. I left the ship in Stanlow in the Manchester Ship Canal, and my Wife and I set off for home for some well needed leave.

We arrived in Euston Station and were on our way to find a taxi, when my Wife said to me, "Why don't you go up to the British Rail Office and ask them if they have a suitable position in their ships for you?" My answer to my Wife was, "I don't think so, I'm getting a bit too long in the tooth to change jobs at my time of life" which was 40 years of age. It meant that I had another 15 years to serve as Master in tankers with my company the Eagle Oil Shipping Company Limited and as there was only my Wife to consider, for we had no children, I felt it just wasn't fair to leave my Wife to go through the rest of her life alone and having to fend for herself as she grew older.

The old s.s. "DUKE OF LANCASTER" built in 1936 and sold for scrap in 1956.

This was not on, so I agreed to visit the British Rail Office there and then. So I took myself off up the stairs to the offices of B.R. and asked to see someone re-employment in British Rail, Marine Section, if possible. I was shown into an office and introduced to a Mr. Cope and Mr. Riley, who asked what I wanted. I told them that I had served in tankers for $22^1/_2$ years and felt I had had enough deep sea and would like to serve in their ships nearer home. I also told them that I knew all about the job, as my Brother-in-Law was an Officer in their ships on the Heysham - Belfast service, and was married to my eldest sister.

Mr.Cope looked at me and smiled and said, "See that letter over there on the desk?" I nodded and he told me to read it, I picked up the letter and read the contents. It was a letter from an Officer in Heysham to the Marine Section at Euston, asking for a transfer from Heysham back to his home station of Holyhead in North Wales. As he had been off his home station for $6^1/_2$ years, for the company's convenience, they were now granting him his request. Mr.Cope said to me when I had finished reading the letter, "Captain Nash, you can have that job." They assured me I would be placed on the permanent staff within three weeks. They requested that I should go up to Heysham and hold myself in readiness to join one of their ships. Three days later my Wife and I were settled in with my Sister and Brother-in-Law in their house in Heysham. I went down to the Marine Office in Heysham Harbour and introduced myself to the Marine Superintendent. Four nights later I sailed as Third Officer of the R.M.S. "Duke of Lancaster" with a British Rail Senior Master, one Captain E. B. Sarjeant an Australian by birth, and as fine a man as one could wish to know. My first sailing was in October 1949 and I stayed with the company for 26 years, until I retired as one of British Rail's Senior

Passenger Ship Masters. My retirement date was the 14th June 1975. I'm very sorry to say that British Rail in all its wisdom, decided that the service which had been running for 73 years was not now a viable proposition, and closed down the passenger service on the 6th April 1975. From then onwards the port became a cargo port and a passenger port for the Isle of Man.

Needless to say, to leave the Eagle Oil Company after such a long time i.e. almost 23 years, took a great deal of soul searching and deep thought because it meant that I would lose my place as a ship master and have to drop back to the very beginning as Third Officer once again, and suffer a big drop in salary. Nevertheless to get a job with some kind of home life, and yet be a seafarer as well, it was necessary to make the sacrifice to obtain a better life for myself and my Wife in later years.

Chapter 10

The ships on the Heysham Service were fine old type coal burners and old fashioned in many ways, but they were very fast ships. They were somewhat spartan in the accommodation for passengers and crew, but they had been very advanced when they were built in 1936. We carried Irish and English Officers and crew and this worked out very well because the Irish men all went home when we were in Ireland and the English Officers looked after the ship and they returned the compliment when the ship was in England. This was a first class way of running the service, as all the officers and crew had the best amount of home life and sufficient rest to enable them to do an efficient job.

The job went something like this, I left home at 2200 hrs and walked down to the harbour, a distance of about $1^1/2$ miles. On arrival on board I changed into uniform, checked the ship all round and supervised the embarkation of passengers. We sailed at midnight and the passage time was 7 hrs and 5 mins quay to quay, and we were usually tied up in the berth in Belfast by 7 a.m. After a wash and shave we had breakfast, then looked to various jobs around the ship i.e. boat drills, fire drills, abandon ship drills and the general maintenance work and maybe a visit to the shore office and shipping office to see our Passenger Manager re any problems which might arise.

It was our practice to sleep from 1300 hrs until 1800 hrs when we were called and went down to the dining room for our evening dinner at 1900 hrs. One hour before sailing time i.e. 2215 hrs, all bridge equipment was tested for the nights passage to Heysham. If all was well then the officer of the deck would report to the Master that all gear was tested and the ship was ready for sea. At 2215 hrs the vessel sailed and all being well arrived in Heysham at 0530 hrs the following morning. After a wash and a shave the English Officers went home and went to bed in their own homes until about 1100 hrs, the rest of the day was their own until they rejoined the ship at 2230 hrs.

I worked along these lines for many years until I became Master, then I was responsible for the ship 24 hours each day, whilst my name was on the ship's register. As Master I usually arrived in Heysham at about 0530 hrs in the mornings, and after putting the ship alongside in her berth, I rang off "Finished with Engines" and watched the passenger gangways put out in place and secured. I then went along to my cabin and read the morning mail from our office, if there was any pressing mail or something that needed to be attended to at once, I made it a routine job to attend our office and speak with our Marine Superintendent and supply any information he might require. After reading the morning mail I washed and shaved and went to bed, and at 10 o'clock my steward called me with a cup of coffee and a bacon sandwich. I then got dressed and went to the office as I have already mentioned. After attending the office I went down to the car park, got into my car and went home. The rest of the day was spent at home or round about the district, if one was going further afield then it was necessary to inform the office and arrange for the Chief Officer to "Stand By" in case of an emergency. When on the run we rejoined the ship as I have said before at 2230 hrs ready for the passage to Belfast in Northern Ireland.

In 1956 we had three new ships built, they were the R.M.S. "Duke of Lancaster", R.M.S. "Duke of Argyll" and the R.M.S. "Duke of Rothsay". These were beautiful ships at 5,000 tons and carried 1,800 passengers. They were converted in 1972 to car ferries and we carried about 70 cars and 1,200

One of the author's commands, the R.M.S. "DUKE OF LANCASTER", alongside in Heysham Harbour, Lancashire.

passengers. The new ships were elegant wonderful vessels and they made over 24 knots on their initial trials. They were beautiful to handle and very, very comfortable to sail in, British Rail always put the best of everything into their vessels. If there was anything wrong then look to the man, the ship was seldom at fault.

For about 18 months after my retirement I was given the job of relief Marine Superintendent and Harbour Master, this helped me to keep busy and up to date generally with shipping. It also helped me to ease away from the very demanding job of being a passenger ship Master, with its demanding concentration and full attention to the job. Eighteen months seemed to be just right and I didn't mind too much when I finally had to "Swallow the Anchor" and pack up for good.

In 1970 I was asked by British Rail if I would agree to having my name added to the list of Nautical Assessors and of course I was more than pleased to accept the honour. The appointment is made by the Secretary of State to the Home Office, for a period of 3 years, and one's name is sent up for reselection every 3 years for reinstatement. I served the Home Office for a period of 10 years and served on about six or seven shipping enquiries, during that time. The two longest enquiries I sat on were the loss of the m.v. "Burtonia" and the m.v. "Lovat". I think the "Burtonia" took 49 days in court and the "Lovat" 47 days. As an Assessor one sat on the court as an assistant to the Wreck Commissioner and gave professional advice as required. Both of these cases were carried out with the utmost attention to detail. Wreck Commissioner Mr. R. F. Stone, was the Judge on the m.v. "Burtonia" case and a more thorough man it would be hard to find anywhere. At the end of 49 days enquiry, no avenue was left unexplored and every question that could be thought of was asked and a suitable foolproof answer obtained before going on to another question. At the end of the enquiry when all had been asked and answered there was nothing left to be said.

These Judges or Wreck Commissioners as they are known on the Admiralty Court Circuit are men of vast experience and have a great inner knowledge of the sea and all its many facets. They were fine men to work with and one was perfectly free to make suggestions or give opinions that one thought were relevant. The case of the m.v. "Lovat" was just as thorough under Wreck Commissioner Mr. J. F. Willmer Q.C. All these men were Q.C.s and were well trained to administer the law. We Assessors made good friends among these legal gentlemen and were privileged to visit them in their chambers, in Lincoln's Inn and The Temple, on several occasions. We had a happy relationship and burned much midnight oil, during our efforts to get at the truth of these enquiries and when we were done, one had a feeling of a job well done, with justice and fairness to all concerned. I, personally, loved the work and found great pleasure in sorting through all the evidence and coming up with a good and satisfactory answer.

I assisted on the formal investigations into the m.f.v. "Ian Fleming", the m.f.v. "Wyre Majestic", the s.t. "Ceasar", the s.t. "Summerside", and last but not least the m.v. "Burtonia" and the m.v. "Lovat". These were the longest cases ever held in court, I believe the case of the Shell tanker "Mactra" was the longest enquiry on record. British Railway management were keen to be involved with these kind of things, and always saw to it that I was relieved in plenty of time to get to the enquiry venue. The enquiry was usually held in the town or the port of Registry of the ship in question. It involved a lot of travelling and putting up at hotels, but was interesting and time consuming.

The author in the wheelhouse of his ship the
R.M.S. "DUKE OF ARGYLL"

In 1980 when I had reached my 70th birthday I received a very nice letter from the Home Office saying that as I had now reached my 70th birthday it was the rule of the Home Office that all Nautical Assessors Class 1 must retire from the list of assessors. They thanked me for my service over the years and wished me well. I was very sorry to give up but one has to step down and make room for younger men. I am now coming up to 82 years of age and have decided to write my life story. This is not an easy task after all these years, but it makes you think, and that can't be bad. My time is now taken up with serving the Nautical Institute in whatever capacity I can. The Nautical Institute is the body that works towards the interests of the sea and mariners in general, I will write about that later.

Chapter 11

With my many years serving in tankers I have always interested myself in safety at sea, and "fire" has been one of my greatest interests. This would be a good place to enter my article on "FIRE" into my story.

Probably one of the most terrifying alarms one can hear on board a ship is "FIRE, FIRE, FIRE." Most fires start from a tiny spark and if undiscovered for a period of time can soon take hold and become an inferno. To create fire one must complete the fire triangle i.e. Oxygen, Fuel, Ignition, all three must be present to start a fire. The ingredient "Ignition" can be caused by excessive heat leading to spontaneous combustion. During the 1939-1945 war, on a ship called the s.s "Empire Grenadier" a tanker, we had an emergency radio room constructed below decks, and between a coffer dam and the main engine boiler room. One day when returning from the after end of the ship to amid ships, I stopped to talk to the Third Officer, who whilst talking to me leaned his hand on the steel lid of the emergency radio room and immediately pulled away saying, "My God, that's roasting!" I felt the lid and realised there was a fire in the compartment. I immediately ordered the discharge of 18,000 tons of aviation spirit to be stopped and all pipelines to the shore to be disconnected, tank valves and plugs to be closed. We then set up a fire fighting station near the scene of the suspected fire. When all was ready, pipelines to the shore disconnected, pump room tanks and valves closed down, we very carefully released and slacked back the eight dogs around the hatch top and raised the lid about one inch. The internal emergency radio room was a blazing inferno and took two to three hours to extinguish. We sprayed the decks and all surrounding metal areas with a fine spray of cold water, to cool the whole area as much as possible, before we attempted to lift the lid. There was the danger of an explosion if the lid was lifted too high and too much air allowed to feed the fire. As caution was the prime consideration we still had over 15,000 tons of aviation spirit on board, we needed to be very careful.

After about 6 hours it was safe to enter the scene of the fire and everything i.e. wooden bulkheads, furniture, wooden decks and deck head linings etc. were completely gone. It was found upon inspection by the Captain and myself, the Chief Officer, and the Chief Engineer, that the fire had been caused by a super heated steam pipe going through a steel bulkhead, with a 1" plywood bulkhead immediately covering the steel bulkhead and somehow the super heated steam pipe temperature must have raised the temperature of the resins in the wood surrounding the pipes, and caused spontaneous combustion to take place. The fact that the fire was detected in time and swiftly dealt with, allows me to tell this story. It could have had a much different ending.

Fire fighting equipment on board ships should be examined once a week by responsible officers, and it should be seen to be in first class order and condition. Extinguishers should be checked to see that they are full, and that the nipples are clear and unblocked and that the instructions are clean and clear to read. All fire hoses should be tested frequently and their coupling threads and washers seen to be in good order and the canvas should be free from abrasions, cuts or any other damage which could cause them to burst when under pressure.

The breathing apparatus and smoke helmet equipment shall at all times be clean and ready for use. The air hoses to the breathing apparatus and the smoke helmet must be blown through at frequent intervals to see there are no foreign substances in the hoses, before the visor is closed over the face of the fire fighter. All crew members should be familiar with the different types of fire extinguishers and their use. They should be made to operate all the fire fighting equipment during regular drills on board the ship.

When attacking a fire always try to direct the hose jet onto the base of the fire, cooling the surrounding area all the time. Two hoses can be used in tandem, one to fight the fire and one to create a screen behind which the fire fighter with the main hose can be protected. Even if the fire seems to be extinguished, never leave it until there is no doubt that all surrounding material is cool and unable to re-ignite. Water must never be used on electrical fires or oil fires, water applied to burning oil fires in enclosed spaces can be lethal. In open areas water can be used to put out oil fires but the area should be cooled as much as possible by fine spraying.

On one fire fighting course that I attended, with the Liverpool Fire Brigade, this oil and water danger was demonstrated. A 40 gallon oil drum, half full of oil, was standing on some bricks out in a clearing in dockland and a fire built underneath. By the time we arrived on the scene the oil had been boiling for some time. We all stood around to see the demonstration, and when the Fire Chief was ready he said, "Gentlemen, please stand further back" so we all moved about 15 feet away, he then said, "That is not far enough, go back further" so we all moved about another 12 yards further away from the oil drum. A fireman from the Liverpool force then came forward with a long pole, a large fruit can filled with water was tied on the end, he lifted the pole with the can carefully over the rim of the oil drum, and then said "Protect your eyes" and turned the can over emptying the cold water into the burning oil. The result was a miniature atomic explosion. Smoke and flames went up in a perfect mushroom cloud for 200 feet into the air, and a ground wave of hot air rushed passed we observers at a great speed. That demonstration will live in my memory forever. Oil and water do NOT mix.

It is well known that most people die from asphyxiation in fires by the inhalation of smoke, rather than by the direct effects of fire itself. So every effort must be made to keep well down below the smoke, the nearer one keeps to the deck or floor, the better chance of survival, what air there is in the enclosed space is always within a few inches of the flooring. It is always a good idea, when entering various spaces, where fires are suspect, to examine all possible ways of escape and never enter any space without a proper backup. The backup must be wearing correct protective clothing as must the man entering the scene of the fire. Never go it alone, there danger lies. Fire must always be reported to the bridge before anything else is done. Never try to fight a fire on your own, report it first. Many precious minutes have been lost by ratings attempting to fight the fire on their own only to find it has got out of control, and assistance is needed. By the time assistance has been mustered, the fire has established itself and vast damage caused, which could have been avoided, if the bridge had been warned in the first instance. Like great oaks that grow from tiny acorns, fires also grow from tiny sparks and manifest themselves into great infernos of mighty proportions beyond belief.

On joining a new ship make a detailed tour of inspection, make notes of all fire fighting appliances and where they are situated. One thing that is often overlooked is the refills for the fire extinguishers. I have seen several extinguishers fired off, and then when they were empty and required rapid refilling, nobody knew where the refills were kept and many precious minutes were lost. Attention to detail saves lives and constant examination of all gear and appliances is an obligation for all diligent ships officers. Everyone on board should be personally instructed in the use of all fire fighting gear, and the individual instructions for different types of appliances must be clean and clear to read. Signals to men wearing breathing and smoke apparatus must be learned by all concerned, ratings must be questioned on the signals at each fire drill carried out on board and several men should be trained to use this gear, in the event of injury to one or two of them or if one is absent at the time of the fire.

Bells are normally associated with fire and rapid ringing of bells broadcast over the vessels Tannoy System is the best method of all, but failing that the human voice shouting "Fire, Fire, Fire" is the next best thing. Always remember, never try to fight a fire on your own, always warn the bridge first. It might be a good thing to say here why we always talk about "fighting" a fire. Well the reason is just that "fight" is the correct word. A fire must be attacked with strength and aggression, there is no hope if a bad fire is approached any other way than with power and aggression. Attack the fire as if you were beating it to death with the water, and you will get results.

There is a great need for a portable or mobile First Aid Station that can be easily taken around the ship in the event of fire. It should contain all necessary equipment, for tending the burned or injured, who may present themselves for treatment. Officers and Ratings with First Aid training must be ready to attend to the injured. Refresher courses in First Aid and the treatment of wounds and burns are necessary, as there are always new ways and methods being discovered for this treatment and it is important to keep up to date. Stretchers such as the Neil Robertson type must be frequently examined to see that the straps and head lines are in good condition, if there are any signs of age or abrasions, cuts or any other form of deterioration, they must be renewed at once.

Foam making equipment is a great asset in enclosed spaces and will smother fire very quickly if it can be applied in good quantity. Dry powder fire extinguishers must always be used when attacking electrical fires, but first of all try to switch off the current. To remove persons quickly from contact with live electric cables knock them off with a large piece of dry wood, or a thick handful of dry newspaper, these are known as good non- conductors, but be careful. Fires often occur in ships' galleys and the best fire fighting aid is a good fire blanket, which can be placed over a burning pan or utensil, remember to keep it covered until it and its surrounding areas, are quite cool to the touch. Do not be tempted to lift the blanket to see if the fire has gone out, wait until all is cold around the whole area - then inspect for fire damage, but not before. One of the greatest sources of fire in ships is the cabin waste paper basket, a cigarette end not quite extinguished and dropped into the basket with lots of bits of paper can smoulder away for some time before really catching fire, then flames reach the cabin bunk curtains, bedding and port curtains, and before one knows it a major fire has taken hold.

Sound centres, radios, videos and televisions installed in ships must always be checked by the ship's Electrical Engineer and his approval must be sought before extra equipment is switched on. Often cabin plugs and sockets are overloaded and this on its own can cause fire. So caution and care are better than causing death and destruction to shipmates and your owner's property.

Bunkering and loading areas, another source of danger, should be kept clean. Spill trays and sand must be readily available when bunkering is taking place, and those in charge must be conversant with the nearest fire extinguishers and fire hydrants, nearby the bunkering station. No waste, rags, or sawdust is to be left around during or after bunkering has been completed, all should be swept up and removed from the scene. An officer should be in full control of the bunkering operation and he should see that, during the bunkering period, when oil is being pumped, that the inner door of the bunkering station is closed and secured and only opened under supervision when someone needs to pass through, to observe the operation. Protective clothing and fireproof suits must be of an approved type and material, and must be inspected frequently to see that all is well.

Ships should make contact with the local Fire Brigade and they should invite members of the Fire Brigade to make an inspection of the ship and all its fire fighting appliances, to see that all is well and up to requirements. They should be shown where all the appliances are stowed and their advice should be heeded for the benefit of all.

It is well known that when there has been a bad fire on board ship, that the fire brigade has arrived, and, after some hours of hard fire fighting, has managed to extinguish the fire, only to capsize the ship. The authorities should get together with the fire brigade, naval architects and like persons and examine the ship's plans to find out where water, which has done its job in fighting the fire, can collect. There are many places well above the centre of gravity where water can collect in a ship, and adversely affect the stability, especially in large passenger ships. One way valves could be fitted in the ship's sides at these known points which could be operated by the firemen from the shore and all water which has done its job, and was trapped in these spaces, could be released from the ship, thereby returning her lost stability and preventing possible capsize.

The ventilation systems in ships must be closed automatically when temperatures in the vicinity rise. The air flaps to the air ducts can be held open by hand operated levers which are also held open on a soft metal fused hook or tie, which will melt and break off when the temperature rises to a set heating of so many degrees. When the fused link melts, the hook drops off and the flap closes by gravity and shuts off the air flow through the air duct or shaft. Fire doors are also kept open by this method and should never be wedged open or tied back at any time. In the event, the hook that holds the door open will melt and break off when the temperature reaches the required heat, then the door closes by way of its springs, but only if the rules have been obeyed and the doors have not been tied, wedged, or obstructed in any way. If all these great inventions are kept in order, and the rules for their maintenance observed, then fire on board ship is well on the way to being well under control.

The sprinkler system should be tested at frequent intervals, and the glass fuses should be seen to be the correct ones, for the space they are guarding. Some need higher ratings than others to burst i.e. the galley, boiler room, and the engine room, other spaces need lower rating glass fuses. Their colour indicates their bursting temperatures and can be obtained from the manufacturer's handbook. Bridge smoke detectors should be tested frequently. This can be done by holding a cigarette tin with some smouldering waste over the detector intake unit, and seeing that the bridge alarms are responding in the required manner. Ships sand boxes must be examined to see that they are full of sand and to see they are not being used for stowing away deck bits and pieces which should not be there, but need to be out of sight.

Drill and more drill is the order of the day, if the ship and its crew are to be safe. Well maintained equipment, clear clean instructions and notices, and everything kept in its correct place, will go well towards making a safe ship. Passengers and crew members should be told of the danger of throwing cigarette ends over the side, without first seeing that they are properly extinguished. All ships moving at sea, cause various currents of back draughts and in hot weather when ships side ports and windows are open for fresh air, also various ventilators to internal spaces, facing into the wind, then cigarettes thrown over the side are a positive danger. They can be blown into the internal parts of the ship, land on combustible material i.e. bedding, storerooms and other spaces where a fire could start, and not be noticed until there was a major incident.

When work such as welding and burning is going on in the ship, a close watch must be kept upon the whole area. Both sides of the bulkheads must be watched carefully through the operation, and the area must not be left until all work has been completed and the whole area can be felt, and seen to be cooled. The scene should be looked over for some while afterwards to see that the fire has not reignited. Because of all the alleyways, ventilators, ducts, shafts and various storerooms, ships are really perfect fire grates and can soon become a raging inferno, if fire ever does really take hold. There should be spark arresters on all ventilator cowls and air pipes and sounding pipes should have proper caps. They should be frequently inspected for any damage and repaired or renewed if necessary. Before use, all portable lamps must be examined and checked over by the electrical engineer. Poor or bad connections can cause fire or an explosion if they short, so do not neglect this duty.

Cigarette lighters should never be carried around the decks and then only those that have a locking device should be allowed on board at all. The rules for having matches, lighters, or any other type of lighting equipment on tankers, or other specialised vessels, must be studied and carried out to the letter by all on board. Breaches of the rules and regulations must be reported to the Master, no matter who the offender may happen to be. No one person must be allowed to do as he likes, and risk the ship and all on board. It may seem mean and unfriendly but nevertheless must be reported for the safety of all concerned on board. Auxiliary fire pumps must be tested at regular intervals to see all is well. One can never tell when the pumps may be needed, so they must start easily when wanted.

F. Find
I. Inform
R. Restrict
E. Extinguish

Learn and remember to follow in that order.

Ship Masters and Officers must know more about the fire fighting gear and how to use it, than anyone else on board the vessel. They should know where all the appliances are stowed in the ship. There is no excuse for badly maintained or missing gear, so examine, examine, and examine again. Be sure not sorry.

My own awareness of fire came about by serving 23$^{1}/_{2}$ years in the Eagle Oil Shipping Company Limited, one of the

"Shell Mex" Group of Companies, and they saw to it that all their officers and crew were well trained in fire fighting. We were instructed by the various Port Authorities, Fire Brigades, and we made contact with them whenever possible when we were in port. When later I was in passenger ships and as Chief Officer I attended a Fire Fighting Course with the Liverpool Fire Brigade, I found this to be the most impressive course I have ever attended during my career. All Masters and Officers and all Ratings should attend this kind of course, at least once every ten years and obtain a certificate of attendance. We all think we know what is necessary, but until we pass through the hands of the professionals we are only an apology for fire fighters.

Modern vessels i.e. container, cargo, tankers, and chemical vessels are mostly well equipped with inert gas systems which guard against internal fires. These vessels are well protected and fire is not a real danger, or risk, with their sophisticated smothering systems. However, this article has been written to cover fires on board ship which start from lack of thought or plain carelessness. An endeavour to draw the attention of ship's personnel to the dangers which surround them in their everyday work, and the manner in which the equipment should be used, in accommodation fires, and fires in storerooms, rope lockers, lamp rooms, paint stores, and all other spaces of this kind, where fires can start and not be seen or discovered until smoke and flames appear.

In the event of the Fire Alarm being given, a senior rating should be detailed to see that all passengers are taken well away from the scene of the fire, special regard being given to any passenger who may be an invalid and therefore needs some assistance to get to a place of safety. See they are safe and looked after until it is safe to return to their former accommodation. For the safety of your ship and all your shipmates, insist that your company send everyone on these Fire Courses at regular intervals. The Fire Fighting Course for ship's personnel cannot be beaten.

Chapter 12

Another item of vital importance is the job of rescuing survivors from the sea. This is of serious importance to the ship Master, and is a subject that is always in the back of his mind. Crew or passenger members can easily be victims of this happening. When weather is bad, people are sometimes washed overboard, or may fall over the side, by accident. The following essay I wrote may be of interest to persons concerned in this responsibility, and may find it useful.

Rescuing Survivors from the Sea

One of the most disconcerting cries that can be heard aboard a ship besides "Fire" is the cry of "Man Overboard".

A human life is at stake, a shipmate, or passenger is in very serious trouble and immediate attention is required by all. What then is the procedure to be carried out for the most effective and speedy results? It is that of retrieving the person from the sea as soon as practicable and treating them for shock. The first thing we must establish in this operation is, are we attempting to make a rescue in darkness or daylight, because the procedures will be different.

Let us take a daylight rescue first. As soon as the cry of "Man Overboard" is heard, then whoever hears it should release or throw into the sea anything at all that will float, to act as a marker, to fix the position of the person in the sea. The bigger the article is the better it can be seen. It must be remembered that the human head when in the sea is one of the most difficult and smallest objects one can expect to keep in sight, if the sea is at all choppy then the task is very much more difficult. It is therefore necessary to establish lookouts as high as possible to watch the casualty until the vessel can be brought around to the reciprocal course to effect a rescue.

One of the quickest and most effective ways of turning a vessel at speed onto the reciprocal course is to put the helm hard over to port, allow the vessel's head to swing sixty degrees to port off the original course then centre the wheel and put it hard over to starboard and keep it there until the ship's head is approaching the reciprocal course then steady up until on course. This manoeuvre will bring the vessel almost into the same water that she was previously traversing. The O.O.W. must commence this manoeuvre as soon as he hears the alarm and at the same time send for the Master to come to the bridge. He should also warn the engineer on watch of the "Man overboard" conditions prevailing and place the Main Engines on "Stand By" ready for various engine manoeuvres. If the ship carries a trailing log this must be brought inboard immediately.

The procedure for the rescue will be the same for day and night with the exception of lights which are necessary during the hours of darkness. If the "Man overboard" has occurred during the hours of darkness then the first thing to be done is to release the lifebuoys on each wing of the bridge, these lifebuoys are fitted with lights which activate when they float in the water. In all cases lookouts must be sent to vantage points to keep close watch on the casualty, i.e. during the hours of darkness the lights are the only marker, and lookouts must not take their eyes off the lights for a second or the casualty may be lost.

Search lights or strong Aldis Lamps should not be switched on until the casualty has been located and is near to the ship or a boat if one has been lowered. Strong search lights will obliterate the weaker lights from the markers and the casualty might be lost. Search lights of any kind can be used when the casualty is close enough to be rescued, and they will also assist the rescuers in being able to see what they are trying to do. On no account must the search lights be allowed to overpower the lifebuoy lights until the casualty can be seen with the naked eye. Strong search lights could render the lifebuoy lights invisible to any lookout. The search lights are only useful to effect the actual rescue from the sea, when people will need to see what they are doing.

During the manoeuvring of the vessel back to the position of the casualty, a boat party under the command of a qualified lifeboat man, should be cleared away ready to be released as soon as the Master has manoeuvred the vessel into a suitable position ready for the rescue. The Master should endeavour to keep the casualty near to the flat side of his ship, and well away from the curve of the bow and stern. This will help to avoid accident to the rescuers and the rescued. Assuming that a boat has been lowered from the vessel and has now reached the casualty they should be lifted into the lifeboat either over the bows or the stern and when inboard wrapped in coats and blankets to replace loss of body heat.

Two methods of retrieving a person from the sea quickly are:-

(1)   A single whip from a block attached to a ship's side davit head, used in conjunction with a "Neil Robertson" stretcher used in the vertical position, with several men on the whip end running along the deck, the casualty being steadied from the boat below, by a foot line.

.(2)   The casualty can be taken aboard in the horizontal position but this method is better carried out if a rigid bed spring is used. This will allow the casualty to be lifted inboard without bending him or her. If he were injured in any way then this would be the best method. There are on the market special wire litters that can be used if one is to hand. These wire litters will clear themselves of water almost immediately they are clear of the sea. The litter and the bunk spring would need to be used in the horizontal position to prevent the person being rescued, from slipping out.

Rescues from the sea can be helped by placing cargo nets down the ship's side, to reach the water's edge. Seamen can scramble down these nets and help pull a person from the water, from where he can be assisted to reach the deck above. Pilot ladders and nets are very useful items during operations of this kind, also strong ropes for body lashings are needed. A Guest wrap should be stretched from the bows of the rescue vessel, along the ship's side and made fast aft, this will assist boats attempting to make the rescue, make fast alongside. The rescue can be assisted in very choppy sea conditions if a couple of gallons of mineral oil is spread to windward, and the Master of the rescue vessel makes two or three wide circles about a half to three quarters of a mile diameter around the area to calm the water. Should the vessel attempting to make the rescue be a Cross Channel Ferry with a 15"-18" belting, then lifeboats in the vicinity must be especially careful not to fowl the underside of these beltings or their boats will be capsized.

Rescue boats should try to manoeuvre in the vicinity of the lifeboat skids so that their gunwales do not get under the

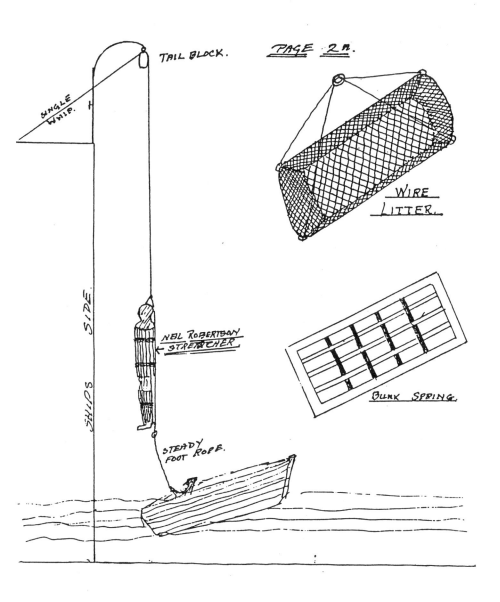

TAIL BLOCK.

PAGE 2 A.

SINGLE WHIP.

WIRE LITTER.

SHIPS SIDE.

NEIL ROBERTSON STRETCHER

BUNK SPRING.

STEADY FOOT ROPE.

J. DELANEY NASH.

119

beltings. This belting is very dangerous to small craft and must be kept clear of, as much as is humanly possible, particularly in turbulent seas or heavy swell. If a good motor boat is being used for this kind of work then a greater margin of safety can be relied upon by all concerned. In the case of Cross Channel vessels with wide beltings the casualty can be taken from the rescue boat much more safely, if the vessel will proceed on a steady course at slow speed when a painter can be made fast to the shoulder of the lifeboat. This will assist the rescue boat to steer out from the ship's side and keep the boat out from under the belting. During this manoeuvre the wind should be kept about 2 to 3 points on the vessel's opposite bow, from the working side.

On one occasion many years ago when I was taking my ship into Belfast, I received a wireless message from the "Ulster Monarch" commanded by another Nautical Institute brother, saying that they had just lost a man overboard. As I was about four miles astern and heading in the same direction, into the port of Belfast I immediately set lookouts and prepared our starboard boat for instant assistance. Some minutes later I observed the motor boat from the "Ulster Monarch" speeding towards me. About 4 minutes later, one of my lookouts reported the man in the water right ahead. I reached the position just a little ahead of the motor boat and circled around the man who was quite alert and upright in the water. The boat from the "Ulster Monarch" soon effected a rescue and we found out afterwards that the man rescued was unhurt and was wearing a heavily oiled fisherman's jersey which had helped in keeping him afloat.

Depending on where the "Man Overboard" is taking place, several things have to be taken into cognizance. If well out in the open sea a person has gone overboard then the rescue is almost certainly up to the ship involved. Help from an outside source is usually not available for many hours, so the rescue must be self effective.

If, however, a man goes overboard in reasonably near or inshore waters, then outside help may be of great assistance in effecting a rescue. Help will not come from ashore or anywhere else unless proper communications have been set up and local stations and other nearby ships notified of the situation prevailing. Shore stations must be advised of the exact position and time of the incident, whether the casualty is in sight or not. Also advise if the casualty has any visual marks, such as highly coloured clothes or at night-time, if lights of any kind have been released in his vicinity. Wind direction and speed of drift if known can also help the rescuers. It is also advisable to find out from the engine room the temperature of the sea water. Hypothermia being of prime importance when dealing with submerged persons. If the casualty is taken from the water unconscious then he must be carefully examined. See his air passages are clear and remove false teeth from his mouth. Warmth is very necessary and blankets, covered hot water bottles etc. must be made ready. He must be examined for fractures or deep cuts which must be cleaned and bleeding stopped as soon as possible. Ship's personnel who are familiar with First Aid should be used for this treatment. As soon as convenient all wet clothing should be removed from the casualty, who should be well rubbed down and made dry to increase body heat as soon as possible. Once the circulation has been assisted then the person will soon reach his normal temperature, as long as there are no unforeseen complications. There should be warm dry clothing ready to hand in case he has to be taken ashore by helicopter to hospital. The rules for dealing with helicopters during rescue work must be closely observed by the Masters of the vessels who are assisting in the search and rescue. Up draught from ships can have a drastic effect upon helicopters and Masters must obey any requests from the pilots during the rescue.

There are few persons who could withstand an experience of this kind without suffering shock either mild or severe. Pale skin, feeling cold to the touch and cold damp perspiration are all signs of shock. Breathing may be shallow and slow with sighing and yawning, the pulse is usually weak and the casualty may seem to be anxious and worried. During this period the person should be kept quiet, laid down with the feet a little higher than the head. See all clothing is loosened around the neck, chest and waist, and he should be kept warm and dry. Medical advice should be called for as soon as possible. Even if the casualty feels well, a check up is always a good precaution.

It is always a good idea to keep the ship's company on its toes, mock rescues can make an exercise and various person's ideas can be examined to see what better ways we can adopt during these very difficult conditions. Very often lots of good ideas come from the meeting of many minds, and one must always remember the wise words from the Holy Bible i.e. "Out of the mouths of babes and sucklings came forth wisdom". Often one person will see something that no one else has ever seen or thought of before. From these ideas new methods are born to the advantage of all.

Here I think is a good place to mention an actual experience by my cousin, long since passed on. He was an apprentice on a Tramp Steamer out of the River Tyne and one afternoon when he was engaged in painting the handrails around the poop deck he accidentally fell overboard because a rail gate had not been properly hooked in place and it swung outboard with him holding on to it. He fell head first into the sea and a moment later surfaced and was able to grab the log line which was trailing over the stern. He was only able to hold on for a few minutes because the log line was cutting into his hands. Those few minutes saved his life because he was able to wriggle his feet and free himself of his heavy sea boots. He shouted out as loud as he was able but no one on board heard him. As soon as he was clear of his boots he let go the log line and watched with terror as his ship went way out of his sight. About an hour and a half after he had fallen overboard, the bo'sun went along to the poop to tell him to knock off for smoko but he was not to be seen and the picture told its own story. The bridge was alerted and the Master told. The vessel was turned around onto a reciprocal course and the search commenced. At 1720 hrs my cousin was sighted and rescued. Apart from being very cold, he was unhurt in any way. This episode took place off Durban, South Africa and the only thing that caused any trouble was the great Albatross swooping down and trying to peck at his head. He always had a nightmare horror of these great birds swooping down inches from his unprotected head and face. Good calm weather and a smooth sea surface, helped a rescue which could have gone very wrong had the weather conditions been different. Had the Master not gone back far enough then the story would have had another ending.

At sea men's lives depend upon each other. Good debate among the ship's company, well organised drills and speed are vital in successful rescue attempts. Many successful operations are due to good attention to ship's maintenance and regular attention to all working parts. Grease and oil on all working parts and frequent checking and working of all gear pertaining to L.S.A. will, if needed, one day pay off and save a life or lives. Great satisfaction can be felt from that thought alone, when one is engaged in tedious and dirty jobs. Even if only one life is saved in 20 years then all the work involved will have been well worth any trouble incurred.

During my fifty years at sea I have always been astonished by the way many people act in a situation of dire emergency. People who seem to be afraid of their own shadows, show up as lions and very inventive lions at that. They seem to acquire strength and vision from out of the fresh air. One saw it during the last war on many different occasions and felt proud to know them.

To finally sum up "Rescuing Survivors from the Sea" this will rely upon good lookouts, quick action, good organising ability, good communications, free easy running and well looked after gear, good command and thorough knowledge of all that is expected of them. And at the end of the day, the knowledge that another of God's creatures has been given, by exerted, collective and expert effort, extra time to enjoy the precious gift of life.

Captain J. Delaney-Nash, F.N.I.

Chapter 13

In 1986 I was asked to write an introduction piece for the preface to the Nautical Institute's Book on "Command" and the following article was my contribution to the book.

ADVICE TO NEW MASTERS
Captain J. Delaney-Nash, FNI

Dear Sir,

I would like to give you an account of my first voyage as Master of a tanker. After many years as Chief Officer, 9 years in all, I was promoted to the lofty state of Master. My ship, an Eagle Oil Shipping Company tanker of 7,410.37 tons gross, the m/v "San Ambrosio", was discharging cargo at Shell Haven in the River Thames.

As soon as the old Master had left the vessel and I was on my own, I thought it was a good idea to familiarise myself with all the various ship's papers and the contents of the ship's safe, containing secret Admiralty papers and instructions, including secret de-coding equipment and instructions in their use. One must remember that ship Masters in the old days were very cagey chaps, and were not known for passing on very much in the way of internal knowledge to such lowly beings as Chief Officers. So one had to pick up as much as one could by continuously asking and observing.

I clearly remember leaving the River Thames and standing beside the pilot on the bridge wondering is this really me! The run down the London river was uneventful, and as I had done it many times before, not very strange. We passed over and proceeded on to Dungeness where we were to disembark the pilot. Just before leaving the pilot came to me, shook hands and said, "Good-bye Captain, safe passage, hope to see you next trip." He then left the bridge, a few moments later he climbed down the ship's side pilot ladder and stepped onto the deck of the pilot cutter. A wave of the hand, hard a starboard and the pilot cutter curved away from our ship's side and headed in towards Dungeness.

That was the first time I had ever really registered loneliness, almost desertion one could say. The time had come for me to take full responsibility for my vessel and all its crew. Probably the last time I had touched a ship's telegraph was when I was Third Mate and worked the engines to the Master's or pilot's orders. Here now was a different set of conditions, I was now the Master of the vessel, with none to tell me nay. It was now my job to con the vessel and take her away from the coast, and put her on the first course towards Curacao in the Dutch West Indies. I tentatively put the telegraph to slow ahead and the loud pressure cough from the main engine could clearly be heard on the bridge. So something was really happening, the vessel was moving ahead on a steady course. Three or four minutes later, when doubt had left one's mind, the feeling of authority i.e. command, was beginning to take over and assert itself. One gave the order to the Third Officer to ring full away on passage. This I did and found it was not as painful as I had expected.

One's apprehension of taking command is all in the mind. I soon found that all my Officers and crew members alike gave me attention and respect. I was the new Captain of their ship and as such was treated by all in a proper manner. It was not necessary for me to press home authority or stand aloof from my officers and crew. I found that normal approach to everybody was all that was necessary. I soon found that I was running a safe and happy ship and I am pleased to be able to say that from 1949 to my retirement in 1975 I only experienced the very smallest amount of crew trouble, even though I ended my time as Master of the R.M.S. "Duke of Argyll" on the Heysham-Belfast Service.

My advice to new and young ship Masters is that they join their ship, and, so long as everything is running smoothly and safely, then just take up the roll of observer for a period of time: later on they can change anything they don't like. It is not a good idea to change things too soon after taking up a new command. Very often there are obscure reasons why things are being done in certain ways, and these reasons the new Master must try to find out first. The new Master should try to familiarise himself with all and every part of the ship. The anchors and the cables are the Master's best friend; he should know all about them, even down to finding out if the cables are shackled or lashed to the chain locker bulkhead. He should know that the anchor shackles and their pins are secure in their places, and as soon as possible should make sure that the shank of each anchor moves freely within the crown of each anchor. Good lubrication here will pay dividends, and serve the Master well in any emergency. The windlass should be well looked after and maintained, this being one's prime power for working anchors and cables. The condition of all standing and running gear will tell the new Master just how well the ship has been maintained in the past.

Department of Transport Regulations should be observed, and the Master should be up to the minute with all the latest statutory instruments, boat and fire drill etc. also inspection of officers and crew, and where applicable, passenger accommodation, should be carried out regularly. Inspection of accommodation should never be missed as this is part of the ship's discipline and must be seen by all. Masters should attend D.Tp. Regulation drills and be conspicuous to the crew.

Tests should be carried out with the inflatable life rafts and access to and from the water around the vessel. Lifeboats and their gear and contents should be frequently examined and Masters should know more about them than anyone else. The upkeep and examination of the ship's navigation lights and all communication equipment should be well respected and all laws governing them should be adhered to at all times.

The Master should be approachable by all on board, but I would suggest that he be contacted by way of the Chief Officer first. The Master can and will delegate a good deal of work to subordinates but first of all he must have personal knowledge of his ship and all its many parts. The Master should insist upon the proper approach by his subordinates, and the use of correct dress whenever it is possible. During actual working hours when officers are busy, strict attention to dress can be relaxed, but they should all know that, when able, proper dress is essential to the general well-being of the ship and to the discipline for all concerned. Never be too big headed to consult with your junior officers on matters of complexity, their help at times can prove invaluable.

Make no alterations in a first command until you have proved that alterations are really necessary, and think them through, to make sure. Attention to normal requirements and a close study of each problem will pay off in the end. Never leave yourself open to adverse criticism.

Bon voyage!

I am now coming to the end of my story and apart from the next chapter which is about present day events, the rest of the book is of a technical nature and I hope will be of interest to many of the readers.

Chapter 14

I am now approaching my 90th birthday and spend my time keeping my bungalow in order and helping my Wife with the gardening. We both belong to the Littlehampton and District Camera Club which meets each week, where we have some very good slide shows. Some of the shows are given by our own club members and some by visiting members from other clubs in the district. All our club competitions are well patronised and certificates given for the best slides and prints entered. We also have three or four outings each year to places of photographic interest, and a good time is had by all. I also belong to the General Council of the Nautical Institute and am a member of the Papers and Technical Committee for the same Institute.

We now live in a lovely little village near Rustington and Littlehampton on the south coast of England, and our three bedroomed bungalow is situated just one mile north of the English Channel. We have lovely grass and beach walks to the east and west along the seashore, and wonderful Sussex countryside to the north of us. We are also blessed with a very good train service and our main station is Angmering. The pace of living here is slow and quiet and favoured by retired people, the medical attention in this area is excellent and people generally are very kind and helpful.

Since coming to Sussex in 1984 I have become a member of the West Sussex Master Mariner's Association and we meet on the first Friday of every month for a luncheon and general get together. Needless to say we have a good chat about old times at sea and travelling around the world and its many ports.

I decided to have a go at writing this book about eight years ago but somehow it got lost on the way and I forgot all about it until my niece asked how I was getting along with it, so somewhat embarrassed I have decided to continue the story, with the hope it will be of some interest to someone who may find this kind of writing enjoyable.

I am pleased to say that both my Wife and I are blessed with good health and recently I had a medical examination for my driving insurance people, and passed without difficulty. My Wife and I have taken vitamins for many years, Vitamins E, C, Garlic Pearls and a multi-vitamin. We eat plenty of fruit and vegetables, fish and chicken but not a lot of meat. We eat no packet food at all and our breakfast consists of muesli and porridge oats. I make bread every fortnight and that consists of:

18 ozs Unbleached Flour   1½ pts Warm Water (to which I
36 ozs Wholemeal Flour   add 1 tablespoonful of Olive or
2 Sachets of Dried Yeast   Sunflower Oil)

Mix well, allow to rise in a warm place for about an hour, measure out into greased baking tins and bake in the oven for 23 minutes at 210 degrees Centigrade, leave to cool for about 10 minutes, turn out onto a grill and allow to dry before serving or freezing.

We go to bed about 11.30 pm until we wake about 7.45 am. We get up right away and never lie in. Somehow we seem to keep busy all day long and we never take rest until we have afternoon tea at about 4 o'clock.

My Wife and I always consult each other whenever there is a problem, whether it be a small problem or a big one. Deciding the answer together is always a good idea and two heads are better than one, as the saying goes.

The author and his wife, aged 85 years,
living in East Preston, West Sussex, England

As I have said before - I must soon think of bringing this story to a close, because it can't be long before I go outward bound on the longest voyage of my life, off into oblivion for eternity. It's hard to understand but perhaps one day we will find out the reason and the answer. The Great Architect of the Universe may enlighten us. Who knows.

Chapter 15

m.v. "BURTONIA"

I will insert the story of the loss of the m.v. "Burtonia" and the account of the investigation by Admiralty Court, for those who may be interested.

The Coastguard

On information being received of a vessel or aircraft being in distress or serious difficulty, the coastguard is trained to keep an alert watch and to take action to save life. Watch is kept on all our coasts throughout the 24hrs of the day, visually and on radio telephony, and by telephone. There are ten divisions (these divisions have now been cut down, owing to modern means of better communications) and are under the command of an Inspector. The divisions were again split up into districts with District Officers in command. Each district contained smaller Stations under the control of a Station Officer. Inspectors should be kept informed and have full knowledge of any casualty or incident in his own district.

Coastguards may depart from the written instructions if in his opinion he should do so. (Chapter 1 - 17 Coastguard Manual).

Duties in Distress

1. To obtain all information, and evaluate same carefully.

2. Initiate appropriate action without delay.

3. Maintain accurate records of all action taken.

4. Establish communications with all concerned i.e. Radio Telephony, VHF etc.

5. Co-ordinate the action of all taking part and ensure exchange of information is maintained throughout.

6. Unless there is definite evidence, never assume anything.

7. Leave nothing to chance.

8. Friction, or one-upmanship has no place in life saving.

Loss of the m.v. "Burtonia"

The sinking of the m.v. "Burtonia" with a cargo of lead concentrate was a tragedy which took place at 0337 hrs on Thursday 30th November 1972 approximately 7 miles eastward of Southwold in Suffolk. The Aldeburg Lifeboat was launched to the casualty at 2135 hrs only 53 minutes after the "Mayday" was received.

The "Burtonia's" position was given as 8 miles E.N.E. of the Outer Gabbard Light Vessel. One of the main factors that contributed to this casualty was the fact that the "Burtonia" was moving and was not static, a condition assumed by all. The lifeboat from Aldeburg proceeded to the position given i.e. 8 miles E.N.E. of the Outer Gabbard Light Vessel, and from that moment onwards the whole procedure became worsened, because none of the vessels involved fixed the position of the casualty in a proper manner, and therefore never realised she was in fact moving, and from this, what was really a stern chase developed to no avail.

The Royal National Lifeboat carried out his instructions in a correct manner but did not use any initiative. Never at any time did he question the position in a sufficient way to help him find the casualty. In my opinion too much was assumed and after 3 hours had elapsed and still the true position of the "Burtonia" had not been fixed, then other assistance such as helicopters and aircraft should have been brought into full use. Surely, if after 2¹/₂ hrs or so no sign of the casualty had been observed, and it was already known she was being escorted by the "John M" a reasonable sized vessel, and therefore quite visible on this clear night to all, then something very unusual was wrong and other efforts should have been brought into use to try to locate her. Far too much was assumed by the control, and not enough exchange of information between all concerned. The radio station i.e. North Foreland, should have fixed the "Burtonia's" position and enquired as to their future intentions.

The fact that the North Foreland Radio Station just kept broadcasting the original position as given in the "Mayday" caused others to assume that the casualty was static, and not moving. It was this factor that lead to the loss of life as the Aldeburg Lifeboat wasted most of the night running in the wrong directions. If an aircraft had been brought out and onto the scene she would have located the casualty and saved a great deal of vital time for all.

One factor which has come to light in this casualty enquiry is the appalling handwriting of the station officers generally. Their handwriting was bad and almost illegible and their figures more than difficult to decipher. Log books should be kept clean and under proper cover. They should be written in the best handwriting possible under the circumstances, avoiding scrawl remembering as now they sometimes have to be examined in detail. Messages sent and received are of vital importance to an enquiry such as this, now being held in Church Hall, Westminster, London and every endeavour should be made to ensure as much accuracy as possible.

In the event of a casualty, there should be one senior officer in overall charge and he should control all events. He should call for information from every possible source and evaluate same, to enable him to form an intelligent picture and instruct accordingly. The coast radio stations are under manned at night, but in the event of a serious casualty, they have far too much to do, and are really unable to perform their duties as they should. North Foreland Radio Station asked if the "Mayday" could be reduced to "Pan" therefore influencing the Master of the casualty when he was in grave trouble and his mind was preoccupied with other things of great moment. "Mayday" should never be reduced until the meaning that it stands for has also been reduced i.e. the vessel is in need of assistance immediately, or is threatened by grave and imminent danger. When the aforementioned conditions have altered for much safer and better conditions, then consideration can be given to reducing "Mayday" to "Pan" but not before.

The Coastguard Instruction Manual was a jumble of rules and regulations which were more of a hindrance than a help, and should have been rewritten at that time. It is quite possible, that all the instructions needed for the coastguard are in the manual, but it would require an intelligent person a great deal of time to read and carry them out. The rules need to be clarified and reduced in size and all irrelevant data removed, and the whole brought up to date, forthwith. Then, and after that has been completed, all other organisations must be advised, and given copies of the new Manual, so that they also can update their own instructions for search and rescue procedure.

This is vitally important in the case of the R.N.L.I. as they must be advised of their roll in S.A.R. when combined with C.R.S. and the Coastguard at their rescue headquarters.

The Master of the "John M" did an excellent job, but he should have advised North Foreland that the casualty was moving and of her course and speed and of any alterations that were made by himself and the casualty he was escorting. It must be, of course, realised that the "John M" was carrying a dangerous cargo and could not take too many liberties, but correct information was of importance to everyone concerned.

Misleading phraseology was used during this event which caused a lot of trouble. One must not assume that things are known, they must be spelt out in detail so that there is no possible ambiguity or misunderstanding. "Steering In" and "Steering Out", "Steering Before It", "Heading In" and "Heading Out", all these statements are clear to the person making them and their meaning clear to all, but to anyone else they must be qualified by where and what the vessel that is making these statements, is herself doing, and intending to do, and also where she is exactly when doing these things. There were statements like "Taking Water" which really meant just shipping water and could have meant taking water into the interior of the ship. All these kinds of phrases must be qualified to avoid any misunderstanding. The C.R.S. (Coast Rescue Service) operators were not really too sure what was meant, but their mistake was in not finding out for certain.

Another point which lead to some confusion was the manner in which position bearings and distances were given. Points and quarter points were confused and misquoted E.N.E.$^{1}/_{2}$E. was given yet such a point does not exist on the Compass Rose. Many seafarers and pseudo seafarers claim to be able to "Box the Compass" but when called upon to do so find they have forgotten just how it goes, this assumed knowledge leads to errors being made which should never occur. True bearings from 0 to 360 degrees should be given and distances in miles and tenths should be given from known points of land or other definite marks, when fixing positions. Decca positions giving the co-ordinates of latitude and longitude is another sound method.

It is the responsibility of the coastguard to co-ordinate the Search and Rescue, and to do this they must call for all possible information, and fix the position of the casualty on a suitable chart and keep a continuous plot. A tracing of the plot should be taken and put on record after every casualty incident. The instructional advice given to the Royal National Lifeboat should be placed on record for future reference. All messages passed between casualties and the various units assisting in Search and Rescue events, must be sent out on 2182 khz and repeated by the recipient. If the VHF is used then all messages to do with the rescue must be repeated on 2182 khz so that the distant stations and stations without VHF equipment also receive the information being passed between units. Part information is as good as no information at all. Definite and precise information must be passed by all concerned and repeated if necessary until acknowledgement is received. There is no future in sending out information unless it is clearly received and understood.

On receipt of a Distress Warning, all units who will be concerned or may be concerned, should be informed and put on the alert, whether they are likely to be required or not. As the incident evolves they can be called on, or stood down as is found necessary, but at least they can be warned and therefore ready to assist if wanted. It is no use calling on an aircraft, and expecting it to get into the air in 5 or 10 minutes in the middle of the night unless she is forewarned. So at the first warning of a casualty, warn all and at least have them ready to help if required. Aircraft flares dropped over the casualty, will soon help to pin-point the scene of the operation and guide vessels helping to the area.

The m.v. "Burtonia" foundered at 0337 hrs on Thursday 30th November 1972 off Southwold, Suffolk with a loss of life of 4 men or 50% of the crew.

Ship's Particulars: Official No. 30022.
Length: 169' 4.8"   Beam: 28' 6"
Draft at time of sinking: F 8' 10" Aft 11' 00"
Gross Tonnage: 498.0 tons
Number of Crew Including Master: 8 Persons
Cargo: 558.4 Metric Tonnes of Lead Concentrates

CREW LIST

Name	Rank	Effect
ASH James William	Master	Drowned
PHEASANT William Hudson	Mate	Survivor
PATTERSON James	Chief Engineer	Drowned
NUNEZ Edward Figueras	Second Engineer	Drowned
BAIN Alexander	Cook Steward	Drowned
LESTON Benito Albores	Deck hand	Survivor
TOREA Jose Vara	Deck hand	Survivor
PRIEGUE Jose Pinciro	Deck hand	Survivor

A cargo of lead concentrate loaded into the After end of No.1 hold and Forward end of No.2 hold. Total weight, 558.4 tonnes (metric).

The voyage commenced at 0010 hrs Wednesday 29th November 1972 by Keadby Wharf, Lincolnshire. The Pilot was Mr. T. A. Palmer who disembarked at 0245 hrs in the Hull Roads.

0750 hrs: Inner Dowsing L.V. 2 miles off Starboard Quarter.

1700 hrs: Cross Sands L.V. Northward Wind S.W.6 Mod. sea.

2000 hrs: Two heavy seas struck the vessel on the starboard side, probably on the bridge front bulkhead.

2005 hrs: Outer Gabbard L.V. seen bearing approx. S.W. magnetic and 10 miles distance.

2015 hrs: Took heavy sea on starboard side and developed 5 - 10 degrees permanent list to starboard. Vessel remaining at this list and continuing to roll about same, but never again returning to the upright. Steering now heavier than usual. Vessel now steering in towards the Outer Gabbard L.V. List increasing.

2040 hrs: Distress warning signal "Mayday" sent out at 2182 khz and was received by Walton-on-the-Naze (Thames) and passed to North Foreland Radio Station, who took over control of communications. British ship "John M" close by and assisting with radio messages from the m/v "Burtonia". Weather now W.S.Wly Force 9 with rough sea.

0337 hrs: Thursday 30th November 1972 vessel sank with loss of four lives.

In our opinion, due to the last two lorry loads of lead concentrate being wetter than the previous loads delivered to the ship, and therefore probably above the safety limit of moisture content, this portion amounting to about 28 tonnes or so, shifted when the vessel was struck by the first heavy sea on the starboard side. I suggest that the violent jar caused the top of the pile to jerk off to starboard and into the void at the ship's

141

side. Once the cargo had started to move the list slowly increased, and with the vessel working in a rough sea, yawing, corkscrewing and rolling, the remainder of the cargo slowly moved over to the starboard side. When finally the "Burtonia" tried to turn towards the coast, she became beam on to the sea and wind, and listed all the more. Throughout all this time the vessel behaved in a lively manner, thereby suggesting that she had not taken any water inboard into her holds. When she finally listed so far as to dip her masts into the water, then it is suspected that the water pressure on the ventilator canvas covers, caused them to collapse inwards and allow the fast ingress of the sea. As these ventilators were 12.5" in diameter they would act as two large filling pipes, and rapidly remove the remaining buoyancy and cause the vessel to sink. The fact that there were two such ventilators, one at each end of the main cargo space, caused the vessel to fill evenly and sink whilst remaining horizontal.

This cargo of lead concentrates is a very dangerous cargo to carry by sea, owing to its tendency to suddenly turn to slurry and become unstable. There was a report of a tremendous "Bang" from the inside of the ship when she was well listed. This may have been caused by the temporary athwartship bulkhead giving way, under the moving weight of the shifting cargo. There was no question of the vessel not being in good structural condition as the firm's Chief Engineer paid careful attention to his duties surveying and inspecting.

Weather:- Throughout the whole of this foundering the weather was bad with strong winds and rough sea running. Owing to this, Search and Rescue was made more difficult for everyone concerned. Visibility was good, mostly very good, but there were a great number of rain squalls which rendered visibility more difficult during these times.

Gorleston Coastguard Station

The Officers at the above station, although doing a good job of plotting and instructing the lifeboat, nevertheless failed to instruct the lifeboat as to what the casualty was actually doing. They failed to find out four important points and were therefore all led into a false view of the situation. The points in question i.e. Shipping Casualty, which needed to be established were as follows:-

1. The actual position of the casualty, i.e. Bearing and Distance from a known point or place. If possible a Decca Fix or Latitude and Longitude. These to be checked and repeated to all concerned.

2. The course of the casualty. To be made clear to all.

3. The speed of the vessel over the ground, or her direction of drift and speed. This was seen to be of vital importance.

4. Also required to be known, the future intentions of the casualty's Master or the person in charge. Any alteration of plan or the general conditions around the vessel, to be advised to all.

Had Gorleston established the above four points then they would have been better able to instruct the R.N.I. lifeboat to enable her to take an intercepting course. Instead the lifeboat was always going in the wrong direction i.e. namely to the position where the casualty had been. As the lifeboat had very poor speed, she was never at any time throughout the whole of this incident, near enough to catch up with the casualty. The R.N.I. lifeboat was still over one mile astern when the vessel sank. Six hours and thirty two minutes after the actual launching.

Recommendations:-

1. Lights attached to lifejackets, with reflector tapes, a useful addition to the orange coloured lifejackets of the present. This tape shows up well in the beam of searchlights.

2. Ships liferafts to be placed well away from any deck obstruction.

3. Lifeboat drill to be held at regular intervals as required.

4. An extra man, or recording instrument to be brought into use at Coast Radio Stations during all distress periods.

5. White flares dropped from aircraft give great assistance in rescue incidents.

6. Ventilators during winter months, should be removed and plugs and canvas covers fitted. This exempts accommodation vents which are more accessible.

7. Trimming and Division of this type of cargo must be given great attention and careful thought.

The Cargo

Lead concentrates should have a certificate of moisture content issued before they are loaded for shipment by sea. The moisture content of this cargo is critical, and if loaded into a ship with too heavy a water content can turn to slurry and behave as a liquid. If there is a high moisture content, in the cargo for shipment, then shifting boards should be fitted. For safety the cargo should be 20% inside the safe working and transportable limits, before being carried by sea.

It is suspected that there are layers of moist cargo which can cause a slide plane, but not a lot is known about this side of the subject, some research is going on into this cargo and it's transporting, we understand. The maximum Safe Transportable Limit must be assured before transport by sea takes place.

Proper and correct trimming of this cargo is essential, and if there is any doubt at all about the safety angle, then shifting boards must be fitted. Holds should be inspected and properly trimmed before they are battened down for a sea passage. The Master or his representative, along with the Agent or Shipper must be satisfied as to the vessel's seaworthiness. A certificate of actual moisture content must be given with the cargo, to enable the Master to decide that his ship will be safe in all respects, when working in a seaway. Most of this lead ore seems to be below the 300 mesh grade, to some degree, and this tends to promote flow if the moisture content is at all high.

Bilges must be dry and clean, engine room bilges suctions marked to avoid opening by mistake and allowing bilge suctions to empty out into the bilges and perhaps contaminate the cargo. Hatch covers must be tight and leakproof.

Laport's, being miners of some long standing, must have been aware of the various conditions which could be reached by their lead concentrate, when being transported whether by land or sea. After all these years of trading in this ore they cannot expect to be thought of as anything but experts. Closer working conditions and co-operation between the ports and Cargo Superintendents (London) Limited, would I am sure have provided know how on both sides, that would have avoided a casualty of this kind taking place.

Research by Laports and Cargo Superintendents (London) Limited could have been carried out into the previous cargos carried by sea, and their general behaviour at sea, and in arrival in port. This would have given records of valuable information which would have been passed on to the Department of Trade for consideration for future "M" notices or to update the I.M.O. code, which at present is misleading.

Cargo of this kind i.e. lead concentrates, should be stowed in a ship well below the least angle of repose to ensure cracking does not make for progressive movement. One realises that stability comes into the problem but a little uncomfortable rolling is much better than the risk of a cargo shift.

The I.M.O. code only gives one sample of lead concentrate from a British mine. This in my opinion is very dangerous and misleading as it gives a safe transportable limit of 18.8% which could be disastrous. This event took place, the sinking of the m.v. "Burtonia", yet everyone concerned thought that they were doing a good job. It wasn't until the m.v. "Burtonia" actually sank, that it was realised something was very wrong.

I would not say for one moment that there was a neglect of duty by any person or persons, as they were all doing what they thought was best and correct. It was not until afterwards and when looking back at the sequence of events, that various points showed up, leading to some doubt.

One can see, on listening to all the evidence, that we are dealing with men who are conscientious in their duties and would never knowingly let anyone down. Therefore it is necessary to examine all that took place, to try to find out a reason for this tragic event and endeavour to suggest recommendations for the future, which will perhaps help to save such a casualty from ever occurring again.

We have found that all the information was not passed along to each interested party. This was a serious and avoidable error. Some messages were passed on 2182 khz, and some on VHF. There was a break in sequences which we all know from past experience can alter an incident completely out of context.

It would seem that all stations working on an incident at sea such as a shipping casualty, must be ordered to communicate to all concerned on 2182 khz, so that everyone is kept properly informed, throughout the whole length of the incident. If it should happen that they have VHF also and can communicate on that wave as well as 2182 khz, then this she may do, but only after all signals sent on 2182 khz, have been repeated by all those concerned.

Quarter point bearings are seldom used these days and can cause a great deal of trouble and confusion. Three figure notation is the best way of giving a bearing and if given in True Compass Bearings and miles and tenths of miles, there is little chance of errors being made. Positions can also be given by Decca co-ordinates or converting to Latitude and Longitude.

The following is a condensed version of the shipping enquiries on which I was asked by the Department of Transport and the Secretary to the Home Office if I would assist. The Wreck Commissioners, or Admiralty Judges as they were called, were assisted by suitable assessors who advised and helped on technical problems as they arose.

I was appointed by the Secretary to the Home Office onto the list of Nautical Assessors Class 1 in 1970 and served for a full ten years in that capacity.

The work was very interesting and very time consuming and gratifying in every respect.

| 1st case | MOTOR TRAWLER "SUMMERSIDE" (O.N. 303454) |

My first case was the Motor Trawler "Summerside" (O.N.303454). Formal investigation held in the Sheriff's Court in Edinburgh, Scotland on the 28th and 29th February 1972 before the Sheriff Queens Council, Sheriff Principal of the Lothians and Peebles assisted by three assessors, into the circumstances attending the grounding and subsequent constructive total loss of the motor trawler "Summerside" of Leith.

The Court, having carefully enquired into the circumstances attending the said casualty, finds for the reasons stated as follows.

Said trawler went aground on rocks at a point north side Garron Point near Stonehaven east coast of Scotland early in the morning of the 6th May 1970 in darkness. Engines were put astern, but failed to move the vessel.

No lives were lost, but the trawler became a complete total loss. The Skipper became doubtful when off Fair Isle on 5th

May as to whether the readings he had taken from the Decca Navigator were correct or not.

Thereafter he took no further steps to ascertain whether his doubts were well founded or not. He rejected the Decca reading he had taken off Cruden Bay which showed that he was out of position. He failed to ask the Officer on Watch if he had had any fixes or positions during the watch.

It was decided that the grounding was caused by the negligence of the Skipper who did not make any effort to obtain a true fix. The Skipper used the echometer and saw it reading 30 fathoms and shoaling, he then switched the sounding machine off and took no further readings until the ship grounded at 0230hrs on the 6th May 1970. The certificate of the Skipper was suspended for a period of eighteen months from 2nd March 1972.

2nd case   **STEAM TRAWLER "CAESAR"**
(O.N.185131)

A formal investigation was held at the Victoria Galleries City Hall between the 2nd and 9th days of October 1972.

The Wreck Commissioner was assisted by three assessors into the subsequent sinking of the steam trawler "Caesar" of Hull (O.N.185131). After a thorough enquiry into the circumstances attending the above mentioned casualty, the Court finds that the stranding was caused by the wrongful act or default by the Skipper in the navigation of the vessel and that the stranding was caused together with a mishap in the course of the attempted salvage of the "Caesar" becoming a constructive loss and the decision of her owners and underwriters to have the vessel sunk rather than incur the expense of having her brought back to the U.K.

The Court censures the Skipper and orders him to pay £250 towards costs and expenses of the investigation. Dated this eleventh day of October 1972.

3rd case   MOTOR FISHING VESSEL "IAN FLEMING" (O.N.308530)

Formal investigation held at the Victoria Galleries, Kingston upon Hull on the 13th to 19th February 1975 before a Wreck Commissioner and four assisting assessors into the circumstances in which the m.f.v. "IAN FLEMING" stranded in Havoy, Norway on 25th December 1973 and was abandoned on the 5th January 1974 when the vessel subsequently sank.

The Court's inquiry into the circumstances attending the case finds that the said stranding was caused by the wrongful act or default of the Skipper of the "IAN FLEMING".

The Court suspends the certificate of the Skipper for a period of three years from 1st day of January 1974.

4th case   MOTOR FISHING VESSEL "WYRE MAJESTIC" (O.N.187853)

An investigation was held at the Council Chamber in the High Street, Garstang, Lancashire before a Wreck Commissioner assisted by three assessors on the 16th to 19th June 1975.

The Wreck Commissioner assisted by three assessors looked into the reason why the fishing vessel "WYRE MAJESTIC" of Fleetwood, Lancashire stranded off Rubha a Mhill in the sound of Islay where on the 18th October 1974 she became a total loss.

The Court carefully inquired into all the circumstances attending this casualty and found that the stranding was partly caused by the wrongful act of the Skipper of the said "WYRE MAJESTIC" and party by the wrongful act of the Bo'sun.

The Court suspends the Skipper's certificate for a period of twelve months from 18th October 1974. The Court also severely reprimanded the ship's Bo'sun.

5th case   **MOTOR VESSEL "LOVAT"**
                                         (O.N.160735)

In the matter of a formal investigation held in University College, Swansea; Church House, Westminster; and at the United Services Club, Pall Mall, London on forty seven days between 29th March and 5th August 1976 inclusive before a Wreck Commissioner and three assessors into the reasons attending the foundering of the British motor vessel "LOVAT" of London on the 25th January 1975 with the loss of eleven lives.

The Court carefully inquired into the circumstances attending the above shipment casualty and finds that the reason for the foundering was caused by the shifting of the "LOCAT's" cargo of anthracite washed duff in heavy weather.

The Owner's Agents and Ship's Master were questioned as to any possible wrongful act which could have subscribed to the casualty.

The Court finds for reasons stated in the report that the loss of life was caused by said foundering and the faults contributed to and partly by the defective condition of the "LOVAT's" life raft and wrongful act or default of the Shipper's Managers and, to a lesser degree, the Ship's Master.

Anyone interested in reading any of these Reports of

Court can send for any of them by writing to (H.M.S.O.) Her Majesty's Stationery Office for a very reasonable fee.

The Report of Court contains all aspects of the inquiry in complete detail. They make good reading for people who enjoy this kind of literature.

I wrote this letter to the Government when the tunnel under the Channel was first suggested. It may be of some interest to readers. Jonathan Aitken was the M.P. I wrote to. His reply thanked me and said he would read the letter in the House of Lords, as many people thought along the same lines.

THE CHANNEL TUNNEL

The more I think of the proposed channel tunnel, the more I become aware that not sufficient attention is being given to the aspect of safety in this mammoth undertaking.

Fire, however caused i.e. by spontaneous combustion, ignition, derailment, petrol leaking or any other cause, is a real possibility.

We are aware of the danger of acrid smoke and of the many people that have been killed by the inhalation of smoke alone and I feel that smoke is the greatest danger in this 31 mile long tunnel.

In the London underground system the danger of smoke during fire has been experienced, but the stations are not too far apart and in many cases smoke from fire is able to be ventilated to the streets above the tunnels and a clearance by natural draught is then possible. This cannot happen in the proposed Channel Tunnel.

One can imagine the havoc that could be caused if a fire broke out in the centre of this 31 mile long tunnel. Where does the smoke go to? How is it dispersed? How do people breath during this dispersal?

It is suggested that car drivers and their passengers will remain in their cars. How long does one think that people will stay in their cars if they smell smoke and cannot see out of their car windows. Panic will cause them to open their windows thereby making matters worse.

We also know that smoke rises upwards and down low near the floor of the tunnel will be the only place where there will be life supporting oxygen. People sitting on flat tops in their cars will be too high up above this safety area and will get no air.

We also know that these types of accidents don't often happen, but should one take place, there would be an unacceptable loss of life and lung damage, apart from the awful burns which could result.

I feel that a lot of these things have been brushed to one side and not given enough detailed attention and consideration.

It's no good building an expensive tunnel if an accident in the early part of its life causes a public outcry against its unthought out dangers.

Whether it is feasible to ventilate the tunnel upwards into the sea is not within my technical knowledge to assess, but I think the problem needs great investigation.

Until the safety angles have been considered and all possible kinds of accidents taken into the calculations, then it would not be wise to commence the work.

There is another consideration which should be looked at and that is the train drivers and guards. They need to be in an airtight cabin with internal oxygen supply if possible so that, in the event of an accident, they at least could do their very exacting work without being under immediate dangerous distress. They need to be safe to carry out their emergency duties without danger to themselves. All windows and doors of the train should be able to be closed and locked by the Guard or Driver automatically, so that they could keep personal control.

During fire in the tunnel there would be no visibility at the scene and panic would result.

There must be an arrangement made for blowing the heavy acrid smoke away from the immediate area of the accident or disaster will result. This smoke must be transferred away from the scene as fast as possible. Large blower fans or pumps should be installed in the tunnel to assist the natural draught in the tunnel to disperse the smoke away from the area of the accident as fast as possible.

One can go on with this subject for many pages of precautions, but the average designer can soon see what a problem we are dealing with and how we owe it to the public to think all precautions and problems right through.

Cross Channel Ferries have great problems of their own too, but at least they can nearly always see what they are doing and have plenty of room to do it in the open sea. They are no enclosed inside a hot airless tunnel for the whole length of their journey.

No thank you, I'll settle for a Cross Channel Ferry out in the open air any time.

Captain J. Delaney-Nash F.N.I.

Retired Master Mariner Ex Eagle Oil Shipping Company Limited and British Rail "Sealink" Heysham-Belfast Service.
Ex Nautical Assessor Class 1 to the Secretary of State for the Home Office.
Adviser to the Tribunals of the m.v. "BURTONIA" and the m.v. "LOVAT".
Last command R.M.S. "DUKE OF ARGYLL" - passenger ferry.

SAFETY FIRST

There was one case that we were told of by the Safety Officer of the Liverpool Docks and Harbour Board.

He had recently taken over the job and had only been in the chair for a few days when he realised that none of the men working on the docks ever wore safety helmets or safety boots and this was a matter of some concern to him. He obtained some safety helmets and boots and took them on to the quay side and asked some of them men if they would wear them for a period of time and give him a personal report on their fit and comfort during their working hours on the various ships.

One of the senior shop stewards decided this was a great joke and he for one would wear a helmet. Sure enough the following morning he arrived on the scene wearing his helmet, a yellow one which had been duly daubed over with painted daisies, tulips and stripes in brilliantly coloured paint and he pranced up and down wearing it, much to the hilarity of all his work mates.

After the morning work the men all went to their lunch at a canteen nearby. During lunch the weather, which had been deteriorating all morning, turned to a strong gale with severe gusts and heavy rain. When the men were returning to work on the docks and whilst passing around the end of one of the great cargo sheds, a slate was brought down by the wind and it landed fair and square on the helmet of the shop steward, denting the helmet to quite a severe amount. It ricocheted off the helmet and cut straight down the leg of the man walking along beside the shop steward cutting his leg open, a very nasty cut indeed.

Needless to say they were all white faced and shocked and

the following day the shop steward went into the Safety Officers's office and said "I'm sorry Sir for taking the mickey out of the helmet wearing idea, it saved my life yesterday and I shall see in future that all men working on the ships in the docks area are wearing safety helmets and a great deal more consideration is given to the wearing of safety equipment when and where necessary."

Such is the position today gentlemen, and a great deal more docks and Harbour Board personnel now wear protective equipment during their working hours in the docks.

RIO DE JANEIRO

Several of us had spent the afternoon and early evening in the Copocabana Casino in Rio de Janeiro.

In the early part of the day we had gone up to the restaurant on the cable car on the way up to the famous Sugar Loaf Mountain.

One goes up to the Sugar Loaf Mountain in two steps. The restaurant is situated on the first mountain (it's name I do not know). Then on up to the Sugar Loaf proper. All this is performed on the cable car.

We had stopped at the restaurant and had had an excellent meal, very well presented and served. The cost of meals was quite reasonable.

After the meal we made our way up to the top of the Sugar Loaf Mountain top. When in Rio one really must go to this wonderful vantage point to see the beauty of this wonderful harbour and its approaches to Rio de Janeiro itself. The scenery must be the finest one can see anywhere in the world. All one can say is that it is breath-taking and inspiring.

We had all lost most of our money in the Casino playing roulette and had just kept enough cash for our taxi fare back to the ship.

We arrived at the town quayside where a rowing boat of about eighteen feet in length was ready to take us back across the harbour to our ship's which were anchored in the harbour.

It was very dark as the time was near to 2200hrs. Several of us thought that the boat was overloaded, we told the boatman what we thought but he shrugged his shoulders and showed no further interest.

Some of the seamen were sitting on the thwarts and some sitting on the gunwales and some standing.

Off we went out into the darkened harbour. We had gone a couple of hundred yards when a seaman from my own ship toppled backwards and went heard first into the sea.

A shout of man overboard went up and we all looked around the boat to see the man come to the surface.

After several minutes there was no sign of the seaman anywhere near the boat. He never came to the surface and was never seen again.

We heard from some of the lads that he had been in their company most of the day and that he had put two full quart bottles of beer into his overcoat pockets. As it was a cold night his coat was buttoned up to the neck, we assumed he would not be able to undo his wet buttons with cold fingers and therefore could not help himself to reach the surface.

We never heard of him again and his body was never recovered as far as we ever knew.

At the moment when the sailor toppled over backwards and went into the water, the great statue of Jesus Christ on the top of the Corcovada Mountain was floodlit and became visible all over Rio Harbour.

Only the statue could be seen in the night's sky, it being so dark that there was no sign of the mountain upon which the statue was built.

I don't know the dimensions of the statue now, but I do remember that it is twelve feet just across the palm of the hands, so this indicates a very large structure. For the figure to become illuminated at this precise moment was a very uncanny thing and I think it was the most unusual thing I ever experienced during my life. Who knows what is over the horizon?

What is a Senior Citizen?

A senior citizen is one who was here before the pill and population explosion. We were here before TV, penicillin, polio shots, antibiotics, frisbees and fluorescent lights.

Before frozen foods, nylons, radar, credit cards and ball-point pens. Girls never wore slacks. We were here before panty-hose and drip-dry clothes, before dishwashers, clothes dryers, freezers, electric blankets and electric razors.

A chip meant a piece of wood, hardware meant hardware and software wasn't even a word.

Before men wore long hair and ear rings, before yoghurt, plastic, the 38 hour week, the minimum wage and work care. We thought fast food was what we ate during Lent.

We got married first and then lived together.

We were here before DDT, vitamin pills, disposable nappies, pizzas, instant coffee, decaffeinated anything, McDonalds or Kentucky Chicken. We were here before FM radios, tape recorders, electric typewriters, Muzac and compact discs.

In our day cigarette smoking was fashionable, but grass was something you mowed or fed to the cows. Pot was something you cooked in or put under the bed. If we'd been asked to explain MS, CIA, UFO, LBJ, NATO - we'd have said alphabet soup!

We are today's Senior Citizens - a hardy bunch when you think how our world has changed and of the adjustments we have had to make.

Anonymous

Thoughts of an older person

Remember that us older folks are worth a fortune with silver in our hair, gold in our teeth, stones in our kidneys, lead in our feet and gas in the stomach. I have in the meantime become quite a frivolous old gal, having two gentlemen with me every day. Will Power helps me get our of bed and Arthur Ritis never leaves me alone.

The preacher came to call the other day, he said that at my age I should be thinking of the Hereafter. I told him "Oh, I do that all the time no matter where I am - in the living room, the study, in the kitchen or upstairs, I always ask myself 'What am I here after?' ".

LOBSTER TREAT

It was our Master's first trip in command and we were returning from Cuacao in the Dutch West Indies and making for the River Mersey and the great port of Liverpool, with a cargo of 2,000 tons of Fuel Oil for Stanlow in the Manchester Ship Canal. We arrived off Point Lynus Pilot Station at about noon in dense fog. We steamed up and down between Point Lynus and the Bar Light Vessel until 1100 hrs the next morning, trying all the time to attract the attention of the Pilot by blowing our whistle and siren at frequent intervals, but to no avail.

About 1100hrs the fog started to thin out and about half an hour later we saw the Pilot Cutter coming out and heading towards our ship.

The Captain had been on the bridge all that time and was tired and very annoyed because, although we had been blowing at frequent intervals, the Pilot never made any attempt to come out to the ship.

The company's choice Pilot came aboard all smiles and was pounced upon by our Captain who wanted to know where the hell he had been and why he had not made an effort to board us the previous day.

The Pilot laughed it off and, as a cover up, asked the Captain if he could arrange for four live lobsters to be put into his bath to keep them alive and fresh. The Captain agreed and called for his steward to half fill his bath with fresh salt water. This was done and the lobsters were put into the bath for safe keeping, until the Pilot left the ship on the following morning.

The Pilot then went up to the bridge where he had to stay till we were berthed. There was a sea cabin on the bridge where the Pilot could lie down and have forty winks and be handy if wanted by the Officer of the Watch.

The Captain had every intention of having his own back on the Pilot for not coming out to the ship the previous day, so he sent for his steward and told him to send the Chef to the bridge. The Chef arrived and the Captain told him to take the four lobsters and prepare them for our evening supper. This was a challenge that the Chef appreciated very much and he cooked the lobsters and dressed them for our meal.

It was a great supper and the lobster washed down with a bottle of white wine made a fine end to a foggy day.

The Captain was of the opinion that the Pilot would not keep us waiting in future. The Pilot laughed it all off and said he would increase his fees for future services. Of course he was joking.

I wrote this letter to The Nautical Institute when I was their representative on the United Kingdom Safety of Navigation Committee. Rule 10(c) was causing some difficulty in finding correct and lucid wording to clarify this rule.

Rule 10(c) alterations

Sir - I have been trying on behalf of The Nautical Institute to get some alteration made in Collision Rule 10(c) - i.e. the right-angled crossing rule - and I have four special working committees under the chairmanship of Captain J.H. Shone, Chief Nautical Surveyor, DoT.

The special committee was set up by the chairman of the Safety of Navigation Committee, who instructed us to try to find more suitable wording for Collision Rule 10(c).

To refresh memories, CR 10(c) states:

A vessel shall so far as practicable avoid crossing traffic lanes, but if obliged to do so shall cross as nearly as practicable at right angles to the general direction of traffic flow.

This rule has caused conflicting ideas in various ship handlers minds and many are not too sure what is expected of them, under the rules as they stand.

A new heading has been suggested which goes something like this:

A vessel shall so far as practicable avoid crossing traffic lanes, but if obliged to do so shall maintain a heading as nearly as practicable at right angles to the general direction of traffic flow.

As The Nautical Institute representative on this committee I accepted the above wording, but was still not satisfied about it.

Later and upon some further reflection I wrote to our chairman and said:

'As you know I have agreed with the changed wording suggested for Collision Rule 10(c), but upon reflection I feel we may be wrong and would not like us to be criticised adversely.

I feel that if a vessel crossing traffic lanes, maintaining a heading as nearly as practicable at right angles to the general direction of traffic flow, could she not, if she were a slow ship, finish up-stream of down-stream depending upon the tidal set and drift, but well away from the geometrical right angle. The CNIS would see this on their radars as a breach of the rules, and if able to identify the vessel would report the master for not complying with the right-angle rule for crossing all traffic lanes. If a vessel is obliged to cross traffic lanes at right angles, then to do so she must allow for set and drift to comply with this rule. She would then be unable to maintain a heading as nearly as practicable at right angles, but would have to steer off in order to make the right angled crossing in adverse weather and a tidal stream.'

The reply I received from the DoT stated - 'As we understand it the present wording of Rule 10(c) does in fact produce the kind of ambiguity of meaning as to whether course made good or the course steered at right angles is required. Indeed, there was in the case of the Dover Strait a difference of interpretation between ourselves and the French on this point for they interpret the course as the former whilst we, for a number of reasons, favour the latter.

The working group concluded and I agree with their view, that by using the words "maintaining a heading as nearly as practicable at right angles" means steering a course and not making good a course at right angles to the traffic flow. In other

165

words, it will in the future be unambiguous and hence not liable to differing interpretations.

The question of application in a particular circumstance is a separate issue and it is accepted that if a slow moving vessel crosses in accordance with the new wording she will not make a geometrical right angle course. But perhaps I may clarify the position as far as the Dover Strait is concerned. The plots and evidence obtained by CNIS in relation to Rule 10 are examined by our staff at Sunley House. Only if after making due allowance for tide, and in the case of yachts, wind, and any other relevant factor it is decided that a breach of Rule 10 had occurred will any follow-up action be initiated.

Furthermore, when the master is interviewed any other unreported factors will be taken into consideration before any final decisions are reached. Therefore in these circumstances it is to be hoped that no misunderstanding of the new rule will occur.'

I'm sure this last paragraph will be of very great interest to shipmasters who know they and their movements are being closely watched by the CNIS.

I don't think that the actual crossing of the traffic lanes presents an insurmountable problem, but I do feel that a vessel leaving either the English or French inshore traffic zones and preparing to cross the traffic lanes is in danger of causing undue confusion, if there are ships close by traversing the near traffic lane. The rule states that the vessel entering the traffic lane from, say, the English inshore zone is the stand-on vessel and the vessel bound to the South West in the traffic lane is the giving-way vessel. Then, to cross the traffic lanes maintaining as nearly as practicable a heading at right angles, the stand-on vessel must when on the edge of the traffic lane slow down, alter course, or turn around, in order to allow vessels in the lanes to pass clear or for these vessels to alter course to starboard and pass under their sterns. All of this is contrary to the collision rules, and the stand-on vessel would be severely censured for not strictly complying with the collision rules for vessels crossing each other's courses.

One rule cannot order a vessel to stand on and keep her course and speed and yet expect her to slow down, alter course, or turn around; such ruling makes a nonsense of the collision rules which have been safe and unambiguous for many years in the past.

There is always the possibility that a vessel traversing the adjacent lanes may erroneously think that they have the right of way, or, on the other hand know definitely that she is the giving-way vessel; this can only further the state of uncertainty felt by all involved.

Rule 10(c) crossing at right angles is only suitable when there are no other vessels in the immediate vicinity which are like to create a collision risk. Otherwise the ordinary collision rules must apply for vessels crossing one another's tracks.

After much thought the change of wording I came up with, was as follows:

Collision Rule 10(c): A vessel shall so far as is practicable avoid crossing traffic lanes, but if obliged to do so shall cross as expeditiously as circumstances permit complying with these rules particularly as they affect crossing vessels.

The reason for this thinking was as follows: the word expeditiously means speedy and prompt, and therefore points to a right-angled crossing as being the quickest way across the lanes.

As circumstances permit means taking all close traffic into consideration, as well as weather conditions and visibility at the time. Also that the vessel crossing will take into account any possible embarrassment to other vessels close to, and that she will strictly apply and carry out the rule of the road at sea for vessels crossing one another's course lines.

I feel that these ambiguous rules will one day lead to a serious collision, where we will see heavy loss of life and property and intensive pollution to the Channel coast, involving tremendous cost to all concerned.

Shipmasters keep their precious commands out of trouble in spite of regulations, but how much safer it would be for all if the rules were clear and positive.

In my own personal opinion, Rule 10(c) is a dangerous rule and should never have been promulgated in the first place. It introduces ambiguities which never existed before, and rather smacks of watching too much television - what is suitable for children crossing the road cannot be considered in anyway suitable for ships at sea crossing traffic lanes. They can't stop at kerbs and look both ways before crossing the lane; there are no kerbs at sea. I think the rule should be dropped altogether.

Yours etc.,

Captain J. Delaney-Nash F.N.I., Morecambe, Lancs.

In 1980 I was asked by the Secretary of the Nautical Institute, C.J. Parker Esq., if I would agree to go to Blackpool and cover the Inquiry into the loss of the m.v. "POOL FISHER".

Of course I agreed and attended every day of the Tribunal in Blackpool and London. The following is a copy of my report as given to the N.I.

THE "POOL FISHER" INQUIRY

The 1,028-grt m.v. "POOL FISHER" sank in the English Channel on 6th November 1979 with the loss of thirteen lives. The formal investigation was held in Blackpool between 24th November and 6th December 1980 and in London on 8th and 9th December 1980 before Mr. G.R.A. Darling, QC, and three assessors.

Having carefully inquired into the circumstances attending the loss of the "POOL FISHER", the Court found that the casualty was probably caused by the entry of sea water into the fore part of the "POOL FISHER'S" hold following a failure of the aftermost part of the hatch boards on her No. 1 hatch. The failure was caused by the wrongful act or default of her master John Maclaren Stewart, and her mate, Francis William Cooper.

The "POOL FISHER" was a raised quarter-deck vessel (built in 1959) with a forecastle and poop with engine and accommodation aft. She had a single hold divided by a timber transverse bulkhead. There were two hatches. No. 1 on the forward well deck and No. 2 on the raised quarter-deck. There was a small access hatch down into her No. 1 hold at the forecastle bulkhead.

No. 1 hatch had seven portable steel hatch beams, fitted

transversely, supporting four sections of wooden hatch boards about 10ft in length and 2^1/2 thick. No. 2 hatch on the raised quarter-deck had thirteen portable steel hatch beams fitted transversely, supporting seven sections of wooden hatch boards laid fore and aft, and similar in construction and size to those on No. 1 hatch.

Both hatches were secured by tarpaulins, batten bars, wooden wedges and locking wires. Cleats were fitted for wedging as well as bottlescrews for the locking wires in appropriate positions for applying two locking wires to each section of hatch boards.

The life-saving equipment of the vessel included two wooden lifeboats for twenty one persons, two RFD ten-man inflatable rubber life rafts, eighteen life-jackets and eight life-buoys. She was in class and her certification was all in order. She had passed a special survey in February 1977 and an annual survey and inspection in 1979.

At her last annual survey she had a full set of twenty two locking hatch wires for her hatches. In February 1979 three hull plates were renewed in way of the fore peak and No. 1 double bottom tanks. The new plates were welded instead of being rivetted as leaking rivets had previously caused trouble. The new welding plates extended into the fore part of her hold under he No. 1 hatch.

Bulk muriate of potash

On 3rd November 1979 the "POOL FISHER" arrived from Norway in ballast to load a cargo of muriate of potash in bulk. She was manned by a crew of fourteen under the command of Captain John Maclaren Stewart, holder of a British foreign-going master mariner's certificate, and was carrying the wife of the chief engineer as a passenger. While she was berthing at Hamburg, she may have bumped the quay but it was not thought that the vessel suffered any appreciable damage from that contact.

Expert evidence was given about the characteristics of muriate potash in bulk. In the dry state the cargo of potash would be unlikely to shift at slope angles of less than 36°. After exposure to high humidity it forms a crust and, with time, may develop cohesion and tend to cake throughout. In that condition the limiting angle in model test is of the order of 40°. Obviously those parameters are likely to be affected by cargo stowage conditions, ship's motion and vibration. Those factors were tested and slope failure occurred with dry encrusted material at angles of less than 30°. The tests carried out were helpful to the Court, but not conclusive in view of the limitations and scale of the apparatus used.

At about 1300hrs on 3rd November 1979 the "POOL FISHER" sailed from Hamburg bound for Runcorn and laden with a cargo of 1,250 tonnes of muriate of potash in bulk. Some 400 tonnes were loaded forward of the bulkhead in her hold and 850 tonnes abaft it. Having carefully considered all evidence as to her draught it was found that she sailed about on even keel and with her after peak full. Her fore peak was empty. On that draught she had only 1.7ft of freeboard in way of the welldeck, where her No. 1 hatch was situated. Evidence of previous voyages with similar amounts of bulk cargo indicated that she would normally have been trimmed by the stern by about 2ft.

The weather forecast for sea areas German Bight, Humber and Thames issued at 1255hrs on 3rd November 1979 was *South West 6 or 7 occasionally 8, rain at times, moderate visibility with fog patches.*

Properly battened down?

One of the most important questions was whether the "POOL FISHER" was properly battened down when she left the River Elbe. The pilot, Mr. Schade, stated: 'All had been made fast and I believe, although I cannot be certain about this, that there were some six locking wires on No. 1 hatch and some ten or twelve on No. 2.' He also added that the ship was down by the head.

Against that statement, both the survivors, Efficient Deck Hands Crane and Fook, stated that there only three locking wires on No. 1 hatch and only four wires on No. 2 hatch. Both these men had been engaged in battening down the hatches. Their evidence was tested with the utmost care. The Court was left in no doubt that they were truthful witnesses and that their recollection was correct. The Court also accepted their evidence that some of the cleats on No. 1 hatch were weak and some difficulty was experienced with securing wedges.

The "POOL FISHER" was owned and operated by James Fisher & Sons Limited, a firm of high repute, well staffed with expert marine personnel, their managing director himself being a fully qualified foreign-going master mariner and port operator of some standing. Fisher keep about one superintendent to four ships, so there is good continuity and close attention to all their needs at all times. The ships are frequently visited around the various ports.

At her last survey the "POOL FISHER" had a full compliment of twenty two hatch locking wires. There were no spare locking wires on board, but there was plenty of spare wire to make them. When she put to sea on 3rd November 1979 she had a full set of locking wires on board and gale warnings were being given out for the area. There should have been eight locking wires on No. 1 hatch, but the Court found that there were only three, the middle one of which was not fully tensioned. Apart from that, it was found that the "POOL FISHER" was seaworthy when she sailed and fully battened down in all respects.

About 2030hrs on 3rd November 1979 the "POOL FISHER" reached the open sea and set course towards the Dover Strait and English Channel. The wind was from ahead, about force 7, and she was pitching. Fully laden and trimmed as she was, she was proving difficult to steer and yawed as much as 15° to either side of her course. The gyro compass failed and steering thereafter was by magnetic compass. During this period the cargo under her No. 1 hatch may have tended to settle forward and consumption of fuel and stores would have resulted in a gradual increase in her forward draught of not more than 3 in.

Tarpaulins resecured

During the 4 to 8 watch on the morning of 5th November the tarpaulins at the after end of No. 1 hatch had to be resecured. The two survivors were not on watch and that fact depends on hearsay evidence, but it is partly corroborated by the fact that after the incident the master saw fit to contact his owner's office and asked for arrangements to be made for repairing cleats on arrival at Runcorn.

There was evidence that after that incident the deck flood lights were switched on from time to time during the hours of darkness, presumably to inspect the hatches and dunnage which had broken from its lashings and been swept up on to No. 2 hatch.

The master ordered three new tarpaulins because he had no spares. He expressly stated that all his existing tarpaulins were okay. New tarpaulins had in fact been ordered before the

"POOL FISHER" left Hamburg. He also stated that all was well and that there were no problems on board, but that some cleats on the after end of No. 1 hatch needed attention on arrival at Runcorn, as well as the gyro compass.

It was not considered that the forward draught of the "POOL FISHER" had increased appreciably up to this point in the voyage. There may have been some increase in the forward draught either due to cargo settling forward because of the continuous pitching of the vessel, coupled with hull vibration, or by some water entering her chain locker and forecastle spaces or through her spurling pipes. (The cement and packing for the spurling pipes was made ready, but may not have been used or may have been used and washed out before it had had time to dry.) It is also possible that an unknown quantity of water may have entered the No. 1 hold when the covers were washed open on the after end of that hatch. There would also be some normal change in trim with the use of stores and bunkers.

Steering erratically

At about 2250hrs on 5th November, the "ESSO PENZANCE" sighted the "POOL FISHER" about 11 miles to the southward of Brighton, steering erratically. That is consistent with the evidence of the two survivors as to her steering and is typical of a small fully-laden coaster in bad weather. Communication took place and the watchkeeping officer on the "POOL FISHER" said that he was all right.

Two witnesses from the "ESSO PENZANCE" made a sketch to show their impression that the "POOL FISHER" had been well down by the head when they saw her, and was taking heavy seas forward. The Court found that the impression resulted from the "POOL FISHER" being seen on about an even keel rather that about 2ft by the stern and they did not consider that the "POOL FISHER" had significantly increased her draught by 2250hrs, some seven hours before she sank.

As the vessel approached the position where she sank, the wind was probably westerly force 8 and the waves about 3.5 and 4.8 metres. There may have been more sever conditions from time to time. At the time of the sinking the tide was probably on the turn from westgoing to eastgoing.

Early on 4th November the "AELIOAN SKY" had sunk in a position with Portland Bill distant 12 miles bearing 272° true. As a result of that sinking, wreckage and some floating containers and drums had reached the Isle of Wight area by the early morning of 6th November, but there was no evidence that any floating container had reached a position at sea to the eastward of where the "POOL FISHER" sank. The wreck of the "POOL FISHER" was later located and identified by Trinity House in a position distant 6.6 miles bearing 232° from St Catherine's Point.

Mayday call

At 0547hrs on 6th November 1979 Niton Radio received a Mayday call on VHF channel 28 from the "POOL FISHER" in the following terms: *Mayday anyone hear me Mayday going over position southwest of St Catherine's Point.*

Niton Radio requested a better position but received no reply. The Mayday was immediately relayed on channel 16 and 2812Kc in very slightly different terms. On bard the "POOL FISHER" the officer of the watch was her mate. The bo'sun and able seaman Throup were on watch with him. None of them survived and it is not possible to find precisely what happened.

About the time when the Mayday was sent, the two survivors, EDHs Crane and Fook, who were off watch and asleep in their cabin, were woken by the bo'sun, who was wearing a life-jacket, and said: 'Quick lads, get up on deck, she's going down by the head.'

Both men hastily grabbed some clothes and together with other members of the crew followed the bo'sun up on deck. The passage was made very difficult however, because as they proceeded through the accommodation the "POOL FISHER" listed progressively to port. When they finally reached the starboard side of the cross alleyway forward of the officers' mess room the bo'sun shouted 'she's going'. Mr Crane was swept into the sea by water. Mr Fook, who was just ahead of Mr Crane managed to make his way up to the boat deck level.

Mr Fook's evidence was very graphic and described a vessel sinking by the head and listing increasingly to port as a result of free-surface effects.

After escaping from below, Mr Fook saw the second engineer, the chief engineer and his wife all wearing life-jackets. EDHs Crane and Fook were not wearing life-jackets. Mr Fook climbed up on to the starboard side of the accommodation just below the starboard navigation light. From that position Mr Fook was washed into the sea and soon afterwards the "POOL FISHER" sank below the waves.

After the "POOL FISHER" sank, the search and rescue services acted with commendable promptness and courage. All concerned, including the Fleet Air Arm crews who actually saved the lives of Mr Crane and Mr Fook, are to be complimented on their efforts. There were no other survivors.

Cause of sinking

What caused the "POOL FISHER" to sink? In attempting to answer that question the Court's task was very difficult because the only survivors were the efficient deck hands, who

176

were both off watch when the vessel sank. Both were doing their best to describe truthfully what happened to them but their knowledge was limited and much of what they had to say depended on their recollections of what other people had to tell them. The Court was therefore obliged to be more than usually careful when considering the central question, what happened, and subsidiary question, ought anyone to be criticised for what happened.

A number of possibilities were considered, amongst which were:

(i)   the possibility of shell plating having been breached as a result of a collision with a container;

(ii)   the possibility of the welding carried out in 1979 to replace the riveting having failed in the way of No. 1 hatch; and

(iii) failure of the end of No. 1 hatch with the resultant rapid entry of a large quantity of water into the hold.

Hatch cover failure

The Court found that the third possibility was the only one which the evidence really supported and that it is the possibility, which was most likely to occur, indeed almost inevitably having regard to the trim of the vessel and the battening down of her hatches.

It was known that she had put to sea on an even keel with a freeboard of 1.7ft in her forward welldeck, with only three hatch locking wires on her No. 1 hatch instead of the required eight wires which ought to have been fitted when a gale was forecast, and with some of her hatch-securing cleats defective. Thus it was thought almost certain that she would be and was seriously affected by the effects of the head sea, which she encountered up to the time when she sank and to a far greater degree than would otherwise have been the case.

Those effects would have tended to loosen her wedges and consequently allow her tarpaulins to tug at the wedges and loosen them further. Once that happened the sudden stripping of the after run of the hatch boards covering No. 1 hatch was not only highly probable but almost certain.

Once those hatches were stripped, rapid entry of large quantities of sea water into her hold first putting her down by the head and then causing her to list and the sequences of events following were just what one would have expected. Neither of the other possibilities produce the sort of sudden emergency which happened. It was thought that after the run of hatch boards covering No. 1 hatch were stripped, the "POOL FISHER's" forward draught very rapidly increased as a result of rapid entry of water into the fore part of her hold. Very shortly afterwards the free surface of the water caused her to list to port onto her beam ends and sink by the head.

There was hearsay evidence of what Mr Crane understood Mr Throup to have told him, when they both in the water after the sinking. Too much weight could not be placed upon such evidence and conclusions had to be drawn without relying upon hearsay. If, as it was said, 'the hatches just flew off,' that is consistent with the impression that a seaman would have got when the after part of the No. 1 hatch was stripped, even though the after part of No. 1 hatch itself was not visible from the bridge.

There is no doubt that the evidence supported the conclusions which were reached, and does not support any other conclusion. The cause of the casualty was the failure of the security of No. 1 hatch which related to the state in which the "POOL FISHER" sailed from Hamburg.

The master is totally responsible for his vessel in all respects and at all times. The mate is particularly responsible

178

for the battening down of hatches and the total security of the vessel at all times. The sinking occurred because the hatches were not properly battened down.

It was with great reluctance, therefore, in view of the high esteem in which the officers concerned were held, and because they could not come before the Court and defend themselves, that they were found responsible for the failure, which led to the loss of the ship. The Court was very sympathetic to men whose arduous way of life and demanding schedule of voyages may leave them tired from time to time, but it was not felt that failure to batten down in a correct manner could be excused.

The advice given in M. Notice No. 666 remains as valid today as it always has, and just as vital to the safety of the ship and life at sea.

* * * * *

Office of
Rear Admiral Fleet Train
British Pacific Fleet
November 1945

On giving up command of the Fleet Train I wish to thank Commanding Officers and masters, and all officers and ship's companies, for their work in the war against Japan.

The Fleet Train had been unique. There has never been one before and it may well be there will never be another.

It was, therefore, with no previous experience and no precedent to follow that we started the Fleet Train, and continued to run it. The difficulties we foresaw were enormous; those we all encountered were even greater.

For much of the time we have lived and worked in one of the worst climates of the world, and in harbours where little or no shore facilities existed.

And yet you have overcome these difficulties, not only because, as seamen, you have been brought up to weather storms and endure hardships but also because of your proven desire to put a speedy end to our enemy.

While we must all be thankful we were spared the dangers of sea warfare experienced in other parts of the world, we were denied the glamour of battle and incentive it gives, so our work has rightly received little publicity.

But to everyone that matters it is well known that in this Pacific war, where vast distances have been involved, the British Pacific Fleet was entirely dependent on the Fleet Train, and a portion of the credit for the final victory is due to every officer and man in the Fleet Train.

The Royal and Merchant Navies have worked together over lengthy periods perhaps more closely than ever elsewhere, and with our staunch allies, the Belgians, the Danes, the Dutch and the Norwegians, we built up a strong working partnership. New friendships have been formed and we have been able to realise each other's problems. This cannot fail to do good and I sincerely hope all of you will do all in your power to keep it going after the war.

Goodbye to you; thank you one and all for your most loyal and efficient services; and may you be re-united with your families as soon as it is possible.

Rear Admiral Fleet Train

The Commanding Officers and
Masters of H.M. Ships and
Fleet Auxiliaries of the Fleet Train